A Practicum Approach to Elementary Reading

A Practicum Approach to Elementary Reading

Timothy R. Blair
UNIVERSITY OF CENTRAL FLORIDA

Edward C. Turner
UNIVERSITY OF FLORIDA

Barbara A. Schaudt
CALIFORNIA STATE UNIVERSITY, BAKERSFIELD

HARCOURT BRACE JOVANOVICH COLLEGE PUBLISHERS
Fort Worth Philadelphia San Diego New York Orlando Austin San Antonio
Toronto Montreal London Sydney Tokyo

Publisher	Ted Buchholz
Acquisitions Editor	Jo-Anne Weaver
Project Editor	Clifford Crouch
Production Manager	Kenneth A. Dunaway
Art & Design Supervisor	Vicki McAlindon Horton
Text Designer	Rita Naughton
Cover Designer	Jo Carol Arnold
Cover Photographer	Edward Arnold

Library of Congress Cataloging-in-Publication Data

Blair, Timothy R.
  A practicum approach to elementary reading / Timothy R. Blair,
Edward C. Turner, Barbara A. Schaudt.
      p.   cm.
  Includes bibliographical references and index.
  ISBN 0-03-051558-0
    1. Reading (Elementary)—United States.   I. Turner, Edward C.
II. Schaudt, Barbara A.   III. Title.
LB1573.B53   1992
372.4′1—dc20   91-15321
                                                               CIP

ISBN: 0-03-051558-0

Address editorial correspondence to: 301 Commerce Street, Suite 3700,
                                      Fort Worth, TX 76102

            Address orders to: 6277 Sea Harbor Drive, Orlando, FL 32887
                                1-800-782-4479, or 1-800-433-0001 (in Florida)

Printed in the United States of America

1 2 3 4   016   9 8 7 6 5 4 3 2 1

Preface

This book has been written for students completing a practicum course in the teaching of reading at the elementary level. The aim of this book is to help prepare elementary classroom teachers of reading through a straightforward, concise presentation of essential knowledge and performance areas. It is not the text's intent to cover all aspects of teaching reading in a detailed fashion. Many fine comprehensive reading texts fulfill this purpose. It is hoped this text will be used in a field-based setting in conjunction with a university classroom. Teachers in training need opportunities to learn firsthand what teachers of reading do. It is through actual classroom experiences that teachers in training are able to practice effective teaching strategies and to reflect on those and on the content to be taught.

This book has five main features: (1) presentation, in a practical and concise format, of the essential knowledge, skills, and understanding needed by effective teachers of reading; (2) presentation of model lesson plans as samples of what teachers of reading must actually do; (3) explicit attention to the necessity of monitoring one's instruction; (4) the means to begin to develop one's teaching portfolio through the collection of sample lesson plans; and (5) a discussion of how to handle situations related to grouping students, selecting materials, and working with parents. The development of teacher portfolios is becoming an accepted way to measure teacher effectiveness. Teachers can demonstrate their competence through producing a portfolio of lessons and routines for the most essential teaching tasks.

The literature on the teaching of reading emphasizes that effective teachers apply different methods and materials in the classroom in different doses depending on a host of variables, including students' strengths and weaknesses, their grade level, and the intended learning outcome. The authors encourage students to take a critical approach to teaching reading and to try various lessons and routines, monitor their effectiveness, then change teaching methods based on their success with different ones. Speaking to this very point, Guthrie (1977) has stated, "If we wish to understand instruction, we must modify it, experiment with it, compare and contrast different forms of it. Merely observing instruction, regardless of its excellence, will never suffice" (p. 955). With today's emphasis on empowering teachers, teachers in training need to think critically about both the content they will teach and the methods they will use. It is the aim of this book to help produce critical teachers knowledgeable in the essential ways of behaving in the reading classroom.

Acknowledgments

The authors thank the following professors for their insightful reviews of the text: Patrice Anders of the University of Arizona; Dick Chambers of Boston University; Michael French of Bowling Green State University; Bonnie Higginson of Murray State University; Sharon Lee of the University of South Dakota; Zelda Maggart of the University of New Mexico; Mary Marockie of Regional Education Service Agency 6 in Wheeling, West Virginia; Jane McGraw of California Polytechnic University; Lonnie McIntyre of the University of Tennessee; and Helen Newcastle of California State University, Long Beach.

The writing of this text has been a true team effort. We would like to express our appreciation to Jo-Anne Weaver and Clifford W. Crouch of Harcourt Brace Jovanovich for their expertise and guidance throughout all the phases of the publishing process. Finally, a sincere thank-you to Nethia Kelly for her expert typing of the original manuscript.

Contents

Teaching Reading in Today's Schools

Chapter
1

The Ideas Behind Literacy Learning

Learning to read and reading to learn have never been of more importance in our society than they are today. The experiences of our human race are recorded and shared through a variety of means, a primary one being through written communication. In our schools, the process of reading is the major vehicle for teaching and learning. The primary task of the teacher of reading is to develop to the fullest in each individual the ability to use language both verbally and nonverbally. The ability to read enables children to open up a whole new world of imagination, wonder, information, and excitement. Students should be able to use reading as a tool to satisfy a variety of purposes ranging from reading for specific information to satisfy a job requirement to reading fine literary works for pure enjoyment. Students need both to know the "how" of reading and to develop the desire to read and learn on their own. The responsibility of guiding this journey into the world of reading rests primarily with the classroom teacher.

Observation of effective teachers and examination of current research make it clear that the classroom teacher has a tremendous influence on whether children are successful in learning to read. Children do not become effective readers by merely growing older. Although life experiences are crucial to language growth, a caring and knowledgeable teacher is needed to direct, guide, and facilitate students' growth in the use of written communication. How teachers teach reading and attend to student differences will have lasting effects on each child in their classroom. Teachers have an awesome responsibility: They hold the keys to helping children find a place for reading in their lives.

LITERACY LEARNING

Understanding and reacting critically to written ideas is of ever-increasing importance in our society. However, literacy for all is not a reality in our society and is confounded by a host of societal and educational dilemmas. Adams (1990-a) reports that adult illiterates compose 75 percent of the unemployed and 60 percent of the prison population. As demographers explain, the future is already here, yet many chief executive officers and top military officials complain of workers who cannot read or comprehend the sophisticated technical manuals for their ever-changing, complex computer programs and equipment. Modern technology is providing a wealth of new information to students. They need to know not only how to comprehend this new information but, based on their experiences, how to react to written communication and make discriminative responses. A more literate work force contributes to both the economy and the individual quality of life. In addition, only citizens able to read and analyze news stories and informational articles can hope to vote on the basis of political candidates' records, platforms, and philosophies rather than their manipulated television images and sound-bites. Another reward of or purpose for reading is, of course, pure enjoyment. The increasing use of our public libraries and growing popularity of bookstores nationwide attest to the recreational value of reading.

READING AS AN INTERACTIVE PROCESS

Although the importance of literacy has been, is, and will certainly remain crucial to our democratic society and individual well-being, the study of the process of reading and the teaching of reading has seen dramatic advances in the past twenty years. Still, reading is a covert process; the mental processes of a reader cannot be observed directly. We use written language to express ideas. Each reader must identify and interpret these written symbols and make sense of the author's intended meaning in light of the reader's own experience. Making sense of what one reads is a complex, uniquely human process, one that has many theoretical viewpoints to explain it. Yet, the focus of studying the reading process is no longer on identifying and interpreting individual words or on looking only at factors residing within the reader. Current research on the reading process has concentrated on the comprehension of ideas. Reading is being viewed as a comprehension process, relating new information to existing knowledge. This process is affected by a host of variables. One very influential view of the reading process today is the interactive model (Rumelhart, 1976). This model hypothesizes that reading comprehension is the result of many factors interacting while the reader processes text. From this perspective, reading is the fusion of various characteristics of the text, the context in which reading occurs, and the reader. At one time or another, one set of characteristics (e.g., text) may influence comprehension more than others (e.g., context and reader). In a sense, communication occurs between the author and reader, with the reader ultimately arriving at the text's meaning based on his or her own experience. The following are some of these interactive factors:

Text Factors

- Content

- Writing style

- Text structure

- Readability

- Type of material

Contextual Factors

- Teacher beliefs and expectations

- Instructional task

- Instructional setting

- Student-teacher interactions

Reader Factors

- Motivation

- Background experiences

- Schema

- Purpose

- Vocabulary
- Knowledge of subject
- Decoding ability
- Metacognitive knowledge

Central to this interactive approach is the use of the reader's background knowledge and experiences to interpret meaning or make sense out of what he or she is reading. Schema theory, emanating from the recent study of the reading process and the notion of an active reader, focuses on the interrelatedness and interdependence of text comprehension with the reader's ability to interpret ideas using his or her background knowledge. Schema theory is about that interdependence. One's background knowledge is inseparable from the text in the construction of meaning. McNeil (1987) succinctly described the essence of schema theory:

> Schemata are the reader's concepts, beliefs, expectations, processes—virtually everything from past experiences—that are used in making sense of things and actions. In reading, schemata are used in making sense of text; the printed word evoking the reader's associated experiences, and past and potential relationships. (p. 5)

In this interactive view, the reader is not a passive participant but an active, strategic learner seeking meaning. Being active and strategic means being aware of how one is reading and shifting gears depending on one's purpose and comprehension. Good readers know how to use their knowledge of a topic to set goals for reading, read to fulfill those goals, set new goals when appropriate, slow down and reread when necessary, speed up when appropriate, and summarize key points while reading. Good readers anticipate their needs before reading, during reading, and after reading, and take action.

STAGES OF READING DEVELOPMENT

As teachers of reading, it is important to realize that learning to read is meaning related and is a developmental process in which learners in their own way proceed to become mature readers. Children progress through four broad phases of reading: (1) *emergent literacy*; (2) *formal reading*; (3) *wide reading*; and (4) *independent reading*.

Although these phases are discussed separately here, no sharp lines of demarcation separate them. In addition, learning to read is an individual activity, and each child's reading abilities evolve in a unique way. Still, it is helpful in planning instruction to know the different phases through which most children proceed in acquiring one of the most crucial skills of their lives—reading.

Emergent Literacy

Parents and early childhood programs play vital roles in the earliest phase of the development of a child's reading ability. Learning to read begins at birth, long before formal schooling, and parents are their children's first teachers. This phase is more than just reading readiness. The term *emergent literacy* has developed to encompass interactions in reading and writing from birth to age five or six. Parents can help ensure their child's success in reading by sharing good books and fostering a positive attitude toward reading. Both actions informally teach and reinforce a variety of essential readiness skills and abilities, including oral language development, listening ability, concepts of print (letters, sounds, left-to-right progression, and so forth), story structure, reasoning, and learning of individual words. Likewise, various preschools and television programs such as "Sesame Street" have similar goals involving the development of proper attitudes and oral and written language abilities.

Formal Reading

Beginning in kindergarten (and in some preschools as well), children usually start more formal development of their reading abilities through a commercially developed program such as a basal reader, a language arts or language experience program, or a combination of these. Both independent word identification and comprehension abilities are systematically taught and reinforced during this phase. Reading is continually encouraged as a leisure-time activity, with text comprehension as the ultimate goal. Toward the end of this phase, readers spend less time on word identification and can concentrate more on comprehension. Readers in this phase are made aware of story structure and are guided to use their background of experiences to anticipate and interpret meaning.

Wide Reading

The wide-reading phase usually corresponds with grades four through six and marks a dramatic shift from reading and learning simple narrative text only to reading and learning more complex narrative text and expository text—for example, math, science, and social studies books. Successful reading in these areas demands not only general reading abilities, but specific reading-study skills needed for each content area, knowledge of various expository text structures, and the ability to seek out, organize, and evaluate new information from a variety of sources. Mastery of basic skills in reading does not predict the ability to read materials with a particular content for specific purposes. Children need to be taught the skills and strategies necessary to pursue the ever-increasing knowledge in all fields—that is, they must learn how to learn.

Independent Reading

The final phase of reading development is characterized by readers who read a lot, enjoy reading, read different types of text differently depending on their purpose, monitor their own comprehension, and make adjustments while reading to comprehend satisfactorily. In this phase, readers are adept at interpreting both narrative and expository text to fulfill their purposes. In essence, they are able to think critically about, and know how to use, what they read.

THE COMPLETE READING PROGRAM

For reading development to proceed in a meaningful fashion, classroom time needs to be balanced with respect to goals, characteristics of students, and the quality of their reading experience. Although each classroom and grade level will differ because of learner goals and characteristics, an effective reading program spans four areas of learning—*instructional, content, recreational,* and *corrective*—as shown in Table 1.

Every grade needs to include experiences in each area; however, time should not be split equally among them. More word-identification instruction and practice and less content instruction will be required in the primary grades (1–3). The intermediate grades (4–6) will have little time devoted to word identification (except advanced word study) and more time

Table 1:   Components of a Complete Reading Program

Components	Learning Experience	Materials
Instructional	Focused and sequential learning experience in word identification and comprehension strategies	Literature books, basal readers, language experience, teacher-made materials
Content	Focused and sequential learning experience in content reading and study strategies	Content texts, content materials, newspapers, magazines, teacher-made materials
Recreational	Wide independent reading promoting reading as a leisure-time activity	Library books, magazines, book clubs
Corrective	Focused instruction and practice on weak skills and strategies	Literature books, supplemental materials, teacher-made materials

devoted to content reading and studying strategies. In every grade, comprehension-related instruction should be the primary focus.

QUALITY INSTRUCTION

Successful instruction and learning are no accidents. Successful reading teachers work hard for their success and know where to put their time and effort. The relationship between teachers expending effort in specific areas of reading and students learning is supported in the teacher- and school-effectiveness literature. Yet, teachers do not operate in a factory environment where parts and products can be replicated with fine precision if only they strictly follow certain guidelines. Any set of effective teaching guidelines has to be applied individually to different children in different grade levels for different learning goals. This realization highlights the absolute importance of thinking, caring teachers who teach children what they need to know, not what some prepackaged materials recommend.

However, while acknowledging that teachers of reading have no single formula for success in all classrooms with all children, we must state that we know many characteristics that need to be applied in different doses, depending on a host of student, teacher, and classroom variables. Still, no matter what method is used, instruction geared to meet individual needs through commitment to individualization will pay off in student learning. To have a positive effect on student achievement and foster reading as a lifelong activity, teachers need to expand time and effort to:

- Cultivate children's self-esteem and self-concept;
- Base instructional decisions on diagnostic data;
- Utilize a variety of approaches to teach reading, stressing all the language arts;
- Develop children's abilities to comprehend text for a variety of purposes;
- Differentiate instruction depending on learning goal;
- Hold high expectations for children;
- Use flexible grouping procedures;
- Design a language-rich classroom that promotes reading as a lifelong activity.

The qualities mentioned above require much time, effort, and knowledge on the part of the teacher. It is almost certainly much easier to stick with the easy method and be satisfied with the minimal results obtained with minimal effort. However, successful teachers take the time and expend the effort necessary to individualize instruction in their classes, not because they like to work hard, but because they seek satisfying results from their labors.

DIVERSITY IN AMERICAN CLASSROOMS

In education, we have very few certainties, but one is that we are all different in a variety of ways. Capitalizing on those differences is what makes teaching so rewarding and satisfying—and at times so exasperating. With the increasing percentages

Success in teaching reading rests, to some degree, on the teacher's ability to meet the needs of an increasingly diverse, multicultural student population.
Stuart Spates

of minority children in school classrooms, we have seen a greater emphasis on our diversity. We live in an age of world travel, global telecommunications, and disappearing borders. Today, more than ever before, classrooms represent multiracial, multicultural, and multiethnic backgrounds. Many classrooms today have students representing more than a dozen languages and many ethnic and racial backgrounds. This situation is only increasing, as two-thirds of the world's immigration now comes to the United States. In 1988, the U.S. Department of Education reported minorities in public schools in three of the most populous states—Texas, Florida, and California—to be 49, 35, and 46 percent, respectively. Reading teachers need to recognize and appreciate the cultural diversity, then capitalize on it by providing excellent, personalized instruction to all children. A more specific discussion of teaching reading in a multicultural classroom is provided in Principle 9. For now, the following are recommendations for teaching all students, taking into account individual characteristics:

- Know your students as individuals, communicate your interest to them, and provide the knowledge they need to grow in reading ability.

- Communicate your high expectations to students and convince them that they will learn and be successful in your class.

- Capitalize on the children's native language or dialect in classroom discussions and material selection.

- Focus on reviewing knowledge and on building background knowledge before every reading activity.

- Allocate sufficient time for introducing and learning new vocabulary words.

- Design writing activities to accompany reading activities.

- Allocate sufficient time for recreational reading to enable students to experience the joy of reading and recognize the connection between reading and writing, as well as to provide enough practice for mastery of basic skills in reading and writing.

SUMMARY

The ability to teach reading successfully has always been of paramount importance. Today's teachers of reading must not only believe in their professional abilities and power to foster student learning, they must also take into account the growing body of knowledge on the reading process and the effective teaching of reading. The past twenty years have produced significant research on the reading process. The interactive model of reading hypothesizes that reading is the result of the interaction of three sets of factors and their characteristics: the reader, the text, and the context in which the reading occurs. Central to this model is the way in which the reader uses his or her background knowledge and experiences (schemata) to interpret the meaning of the text. Study on the characteristics of effective teaching has also been fruitful. Effective reading teachers realize the importance of fostering each student's self-concept, basing instructional decisions on various assessment information, using a variety of approaches to teach reading, focusing instruction on comprehension, varying instruction depending on the learning goal, holding high expectations of students, using flexible grouping procedures, and designing a language-rich environment. Yet, teaching reading is context-specific, with the recommended practices to be implemented differently to different children in different grade levels for different learning goals.

Also crucial to teaching effectiveness is an understanding of the different phases children complete in acquiring literacy; the major components of a comprehensive reading program regardless of grade level; and, most important, the recognition, acknowledgment, and program adjustment necessary for teaching in a multicultural society.

1. "Good teachers are born teachers." Do you agree or disagree with this statement? Why?

2. When it is said that learning to read is "context-specific," what does this mean? What are the ramifications for teaching reading?

3. What does it mean to be an "active" reader? Are you an active reader? What do you feel teachers can do to promote this quality? What are some factors that can thwart the development of this desired trait?

4. What might be the negative effects of emphasizing one of
the four components of a complete reading program at the
expense of the other three?

Essential Knowledge, Approaches, and Skills: Eighteen Principles of Teaching Reading

Part

II

If teachers of reading are to meet the individual needs of their students, they must have a solid foundation in the knowledge of literacy acquisition and in the teaching process itself. This section of the text is divided into three chapters: (1) *planning instruction;* (2) *teaching reading;* and (3) *managing and organizing the classroom.* In each chapter, a set of principles is offered as a guide to implementing reading instruction and as a means for teachers of reading to reflect on, and think critically about, their instructional practices. To help promote reflective and critical thinking, discussion questions follow each of the three chapters. It is hoped you will analyze each principle, examine its premise, and monitor its application in your classroom and that of other teachers.

Planning Instruction

The effective reading teacher:

1. understands that reading is a language process and that the teaching of reading should be integrated with that of the other language arts: writing, listening, and speaking;

2. recognizes and plans for a wide range of individual differences in the classroom;

3. holds high expectations for all students and ensures that all put forth a strong effort in their schoolwork;

4. recognizes that the overall goal of reading instruction is the development of active readers who can both understand printed language and strategically monitor their own reading performance;

5. realizes there is no one miracle approach for all children and thus uses a variety of approaches to teach reading;

6. understands that students need to know a variety of ways to decode written language;

7. cultivates positive student attitudes and feelings;

8. understands the role of assessing each student's strengths and weaknesses in providing successful instruction;

9. knows and applies specialized techniques when teaching students who speak a nonstandard dialect or whose native language is not English;

10. utilizes a team approach to ensure that each student receives a sound educational program.

Teaching Reading

The effective reading teacher:

11. knows the routine or procedure for teaching a story;

12. uses the direct or explicit model of instruction for teaching specific reading skills, abilities, and strategies;

13. designs specific learning experiences to promote critical thinking through reading and writing;

14. teaches content-reading skills and studying strategies so that students will be able to remember, organize, and retrieve information from expository text;

15. recognizes the importance of, and promotes, recreational reading;

16. knows the importance of continuously assessing students during instruction, and of adjusting some students' programs after gathering new information.

Managing and Organizing the Classroom

The effective reading teacher:

17. uses a variety of grouping procedures to help students learn;

18. exercises efficient management techniques to capitalize on instruction time.

18 Principles

- Discuss each principle w/ students
- Use many examples
- Have stds write a paper
  presenting examples for each of 18 principles

Chapter

2

Principles 1–10:
Planning Instruction

Principle 1: The effective reading teacher understands that reading is a language process and that the teaching of reading should be integrated with that of the other language arts: writing, listening, and speaking. The language arts are the tools of communication in our language. Research and practical classroom experiences indicate clearly how each of the language arts supports and depends upon the others for successful communication. Children's oral language development is based on several factors, including concrete experiences and the ability to imitate spoken words. Listening ability is also important in learning to differentiate various speech sounds and associating sounds and meaning with particular letter shapes and word forms. These abilities of auditory and visual discrimination are crucial for identifying words in our written language. A person's listening ability is further related to his or her reading comprehension. Oral language facility is directly related to the ability to read, for in oral language the symbols are spoken, and in reading, they are written. Anderson et al. (1985) in *Becoming a Nation of Readers: The Report of the Commission on Reading* state:

> Reading instruction builds especially on oral language. If this foundation is weak, progress in reading will be slow and uncertain. Children must have at least a basic vocabulary, a reasonable range of knowledge about the world around them and the ability to talk about their knowledge. These abilities form the basis for comprehending text. (p. 30)

Effective teachers design reading activities that integrate the other language arts: writing, listening, and speaking.
Stuart Spates

The relationship between reading and writing, although highlighted in the past, has received much attention of late because of recent research (Adams, 1990-a). Reading involves learning to communicate through written symbols using one's background of experiences. Writing involves using written language to communicate ideas to others. A major similarity between reading and writing is that they both require interpretation of meaning. Writing entails conveying messages to readers through the creation of text, while reading entails interpreting the meaning of text already formulated. Adams (1990-b) states, "Through writing, children learn that the purpose of text is not to be read, but to be understood" (p. 104). In any effective reading program, teachers must design experiences that have a pervasive language-arts emphasis. As a way of enhancing student opportunities to experience language and capitalizing on the benefits of integrating language arts instruction, teachers can incorporate the visual and performing arts into their instruction. The use of music, painting and drawing, dramatics, and film can turn routine instructional activities into creative experiences that promote student appreciation of, and growth in, both written and spoken language. Summarizing the importance of the simultaneous development of the language arts, Anderson et al. state, "Reading must be seen as part of a child's general language development and not as a discrete skill isolated from listening, speaking, and writing" (p. 30). Figure 2-1 illustrates this clearly.

Principle 2:   The effective reading teacher recognizes and plans for a wide range of individual differences in the classroom.   Children need to be taught what they need to know. While this may sound obvious, implementing this maxim requires much effort on the part of teachers. Too often only lip service is given to addressing individual differences. Teaching children what they need to know requires teachers to realize the wide range of differences found in each classroom. Differences in students are part and parcel of teaching. These differences lie in a multitude of areas, including mental capacity, emotional and social maturity, psychological well-being, personal interests, preferred learning style, learning rate, language facility, and ability levels.

Recognizing differences, accepting them, and then planning instruction based on this knowledge separates teachers who attempt to meet individual needs from those who do not. Meeting a wide range of individual differences demands the very best from reading teachers. For instance, in a first-grade class, the teacher can expect the range of reading ability to span from readiness to the third- or fourth-grade level. In grade three, the span can be from first- through sixth-grade levels, and in grade six, from second-grade through high-school ability. Thus, not only is the range of ability wide in each grade, necessitating individual attention, but in each successive grade, the range of reading ability increases. Add to this factor any one or two of the aforementioned areas of difference, and you will see why teaching is a serious business

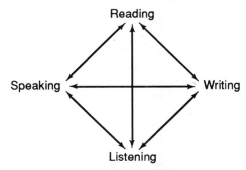

Figure 2-1   The interrelation and interdependence of the language arts.

requiring careful decisions. If all instruction could be the same for all children in each grade, teaching reading would be easy. The acceptance of differences automatically increases the complexity of the teaching/learning process.

How do teachers of reading handle the many differences in their classrooms? Successful teachers implement planning guidelines that include the following:

- Plan for a variety of activities around the language arts—reading, writing, speaking, and listening—to capitalize on different students' strengths.

- Devise and design alternative teaching methods to increase student involvement.

- Group students in a variety of ways to encourage peer-tutoring and cooperation.

- Supplement the reading-language arts curriculum with a variety of materials to increase the quantity and quality of instructional options for students.

Specific ways to teach children what they need to know are endless. Teachers of reading *must* realize that capitalizing on differences is an indispensable aspect of their profession. How successful one is in differentiating instruction will be seen in how much children progress in their reading and writing.

Principle 3: The effective reading teacher holds high expectations for all students and ensures that all put forth a strong effort in their schoolwork. A teacher's feelings about how well a student can and should perform on a given task can have a powerful effect on the eventual outcome. Many times a teacher's expectation becomes a self-fulfilling prophecy; students sense what is expected of them and behave accordingly. Research on the negative effects of low expectations on students is quite revealing (Good & Brophy, 1987). Among their findings: Students of whom little is expected often receive less instruction, help, praise, and eye contact, but more criticism. Effective teachers hold high academic expectations for their students and communicate these high expectations to the students themselves. These teachers believe in themselves and, regardless of student home and background factors, in their students as well.

Effective teachers also make sure their students put forth great effort to become active, strategic readers. Thus, effective reading teachers see to it that their students work as hard on their schoolwork as teachers work on their teaching. Teachers do this in a positive fashion directed at specific learning goals. Central to this is changing the reward structure in the classroom from one stressing competitiveness to one stressing cooperation and individual achievement (Johnson & Johnson, 1974). When this change is effected, students perceive a better chance of success and also see the value of individual effort. To help make sure that they have high expectations for all students and that individual effort is encouraged, teachers of reading should consider the following points:

- Base instructional decisions on assessment information.
- Design activities so all students are involved in learning.
- Make sure all students participate in reading and language arts activities.
- Communicate to all students both publicly and privately that you expect them to meet high standards in your classroom.
- Monitor student work and give timely feedback.
- Use cooperative grouping to promote student involvement.
- Continually tell students why they are doing what they are doing.
- Design seatwork activities that are self-correcting in nature to promote more self-directed learning.
- Provide a grade based on effort along with a grade based on achievement.
- Cooperatively plan reading/language arts activities with students.

Principle 4: The effective reading teacher recognizes that the overall goal of reading instruction is the development of active readers who can both understand printed language and strategically monitor their own reading performance. The ultimate success of a reading/language arts program is the degree to which students can read and understand numerous texts for a variety of purposes. Success is achieved through the coming together of a positive attitude, the mastery of reading skills and abilities spanning different cognitive levels in both narrative and expository text, and, most important, the ability to monitor and regulate one's reading depending on the situation. Viewing reading interactively, how well students comprehend depends upon several factors—text, context, and reader. Reading comprehension is best viewed as a multifaceted process affected by several thinking and language abilities. Teachers need to give students specific instruction and guidance in applying comprehension strategies before, during, and after reading a selection. With the realization that reading is comprehension, students can be explicitly taught specific abilities to be applied in their reading, including identifying facts, summarizing main ideas, identifying cause-and-effect relationships, inferentially understanding information, and critically analyzing and evaluating text on the basis of certain criteria. The ability to read on different levels—literal, inferential, and critical—exemplifies the types of thinking that can be applied to written and oral language. These levels of thinking applied to reading comprehension are defined as follows:

- *Literal Comprehension:* Understanding ideas and information explicitly stated in a passage;

- *Inferential Comprehension:* Understanding ideas and information implied by a passage;

- *Critical Comprehension:* Analyzing, evaluating, and personally reacting to information presented in a passage.

Purposeful reading is a major factor in promoting comprehension. The ability of the reader to establish a purpose when reading sets the limits for completing the job efficiently. A major vehicle to foster growth in purposeful reading is the proper framing of classroom questions in relation to the desired reading comprehension outcome. Providing children with specific questions before they read helps to engage them in learning, direct their purposes for reading, and regulate their depth and rate of reading. Blanton, Wood, and Moorman (1990) offer the following guidelines for establishing purposes for reading:

- Students should always have a purpose for reading.

- A single purpose for reading is more effective than multiple purposes.

- Teachers should use a purpose-setting routine.

- Purpose should be sustained throughout the reading material.

- A discussion of purpose should be the first activity in the postreading phase.

- Ultimately, instruction should equip students to set their own purposes. (pp. 491 and 492)

It is not enough to be able to interpret a text's meaning and respond in a critical fashion. Strategic readers monitor their reading, recognizing when to slow down, speed up, reread, or pause to understand a point. Knowing how one reads, coupled with the ability to "change gears" while reading, is called *metacognition.* Teachers can develop these comprehension and metacognitive abilities in their students by employing the following strategies:

- Always establish purposes for students before reading and train students to set their own purposes.

- Provide guidance before, while, and after students read a selection.

- Use prereading strategies (e.g., semantic maps, story maps, or other graphic organizers) to activate background knowledge, provide information for making predictions, show key relationships, and teach new vocabulary.

- Plan a systematic vocabulary development program to increase students' listening, speaking, reading, and writing vocabularies. The richer students' language background is, the better they will be able to interpret meaning from text.

- Relate the text to your students' background of experiences, and show your students how to do this themselves, by asking appropriate questions using information from the text and visual aids.

- Explicitly explain the various types of text structure and show students how to determine a text structure while they are reading. (See Appendix A for a listing of the various narrative and expository text structures.)

- Train students to use the reciprocal teaching approach of Palinscar and Brown (1986) utilizing the four strategies of summarizing, question asking, clarifying, and predicting. (See Appendix A for a description of this approach.)

- On a regular basis, ask your students a variety of questions requiring different levels of thinking. It is imperative to encourage them to think at various cognitive levels. The reading teacher's art of questioning directly affects students' attitudes toward understanding text and, ultimately, how much they learn. Appendix A contains one possible questioning strategy, based on Bloom's taxonomy, to use in designing and evaluating the questioning scheme. In conjunction with asking a balanced set of questions that require different levels of thinking, teachers need to practice the proven technique of *wait-time*, also called *think-time*. This term denotes the period of silence after the teachers ask questions but before the students respond. Research has shown that if teachers wait three to five seconds before eliciting a response, students are better able to digest the question and positive results occur. More student participation, longer responses, and more higher-level thinking are among the positive effects of this technique (Gambrell, 1980). Coupled with wait-time, teachers need to be equipped with probing questions to help redirect or expand a student's response to a question. To keep discussions lively and extend students' thinking, teachers can ask thought-provoking questions, such as "Can you tell me more?" "What are some other ideas?" and "Do you agree or disagree with the author?"

- Train students to ask questions and find the appropriate answers by teaching them a questioning strategy they can use on their own. (The QAR strategy by Raphael is described in Appendix A.)

- Directly explain specific comprehension skills and abilities to students and practice an abundance of interesting and varied drills for the skill or ability to become automatic. The direct or explicit instruction method, a universal teaching strategy which has been used for years, has as the heart of the lesson the systematic explanation, demonstration, or modeling of the new skill or ability. The basic steps in this approach are readiness, step-by-step explanation of the lesson objective, guided practice, and independent practice. An expanded version of direct instruction by Rosenshine and Stevens (1986) is in Appendix F. Some of the sample lessons and routines in Part II of the text follow this method. Teachers are encouraged to use those lessons as models to formulate direct instruction or explicit lessons.

- Using an actual student text, model for students exactly how and why while reading, they should slow down, speed up, stop and use a visual aid (to better understand the ideas expressed in the text), pause to make note of an important point, reread a section (to understand an idea), and answer end-of-chapter questions.

Central to the development of strategic readers and the strategies suggested above is the important role of the classroom teacher. Only through the teacher's careful, expert planning, teaching, and guidance will students grow into mature, independent readers. This book highlights the concept of differential emphasis on control of reading strategies, a concept emanating from research on the reading process and the teaching of reading. It involves a transfer of control—from total teacher control to gradually putting the student in control of a reading strategy. It is commonsensical; initially the teacher explains or models the new strategy to students, and after much discussion and guided practice, they gradually learn to apply the strategy independently. This gradual shift of control and responsibility for the learning and application of a reading skill is depicted in Figure 2-2 by Pearson and Gallagher (1983, p. 337).

Principle 5:   The effective reading teacher realizes there is no one miracle approach for all children and thus uses a variety of approaches to teach reading.   There is no more complex, enduring, emotional, and controversial topic for educators, researchers, and parents than what constitutes the best approach to teaching reading. The complexity of teaching reading is readily apparent from the following fact: For every approach used to teach reading throughout the ages, a child has failed to learn to read with that approach. Because children are different, there has never been and never will be one approach that succeeds with all children. Such findings have caused educational researchers to hypothesize that the key variable in the learning situation is the teacher. Indeed, although a certain approach may be successful with one child but not another because of their individual characteristics, the

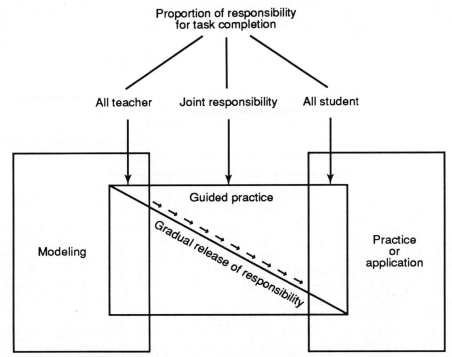

Figure 2-2 The gradual-release-of-responsibility model of instruction.
After Campione, 1981. Reprinted with permission from P.D. Pearson and M.C. Gallagher, *The Instruction of Reading Comprehension* (Urbana: University of Illinois Center for the Study of Reading, 1983), p. 732.

teacher's expertise in correctly adjusting any method or materials in relation to student need is the crucial element in whether a student succeeds in learning to read. Because there is no one miracle approach to the teaching of reading, it is imperative for effective teachers of reading to know a variety of approaches.

The teaching of reading through various approaches has shifted many times in the past two centuries; however, the basis has always been the same—to teach our children better so they will become independent readers. The last decade has seen dramatic changes in how we view and teach the reading process in the classroom. With the rise in interest in the study of comprehension, a shift in attention to how we process and retrieve information with corresponding comprehension strategies has taken center stage. This is in contrast to teaching technique focusing on the isolated instruction of both word identification and comprehension skills. A second change has occurred with more serious attempts at the merging of the teaching of reading with the other language arts, especially the renewed close relationship between reading and writing. A third major change in the last decade has been the growing emphasis on fine literature in all reading approaches. Inclusion of this essential element has spurred a more holistic, integrated approach to the teaching of the language processes.

Four major approaches to teaching reading in our schools are the basal reader, language experience, literature-based, and whole language approaches. Although it is helpful to focus on each separately for discussion purposes, teachers of reading do not have to make one choice from among them. By isolating the approaches in this discussion, it is easy to convey the misleading impression that each functions separately from the others. However, in reality, reading approaches are not implemented in isolation but are integrated to achieve desired results. Of primary importance is knowing the elements of these four approaches and how to combine and balance them most effectively. Each approach has its advantages, and each needs to be supplemented with parts of another. For example, the basal reader, language experience, and whole language approaches do not provide enough contact with fine literary material by themselves. In addition to these major approaches and their accompanying materials, a multitude of supplemental materials—ranging from teacher-made materials to newspapers, magazines, and various periodicals to commercial kits to various multimedia materials to enrichment books—can be used with any reading approach. Another way of understanding this notion of integration is to consider the major elements of a reading program, as depicted in Figure 2-3. Regardless of approach, these elements would be developed and practiced through a variety of means, with the ultimate goal being the development of mature, thoughtful readers.

Basal Reader Approach

The basal reader is a systematic, coordinated, and sequential anthology of stories and related materials designed to teach reading. The basal reader attempts to sequentially and explicitly develop word identification, vocabulary comprehension, content-reading skills and strategies, and to promote recreational reading as well. Recently published basal readers have expanded to incorporate fine literature.

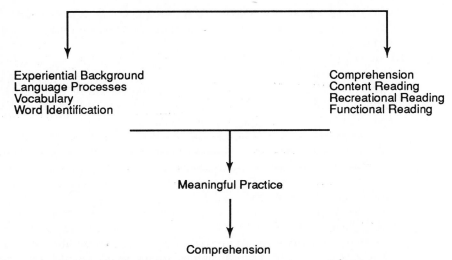

Experiential Background
Language Processes
Vocabulary
Word Identification

Comprehension
Content Reading
Recreational Reading
Functional Reading

Meaningful Practice

Comprehension

Figure 2-3   Major reading program components.

Advantages

1. Provides carefully planned presentation and development of vocabulary, word identification, comprehension, and content-reading skills and strategies.

2. Provides, in teachers' manuals, good suggestions to use in teaching a story.

3. Fosters integrated development and reinforcement of reading skills and strategies in whole stories.

4. Exposes students to a variety of literary forms.

5. Provides a multitude of materials for a variety of practice and for capitalizing on students' learning styles; materials include student readers, workbooks, picture and vocabulary cards, reading games, supplemental activities, computer software programs coordinated with stories, and recreational reading kits.

Disadvantages

1. Through teachers' manuals, may foster an inflexible attitude toward reading development.

2. Is based on a graded system of instruction and may encourage a lock-step progression throughout the grades.

3. If viewed as the total reading program, may limit a child's exposure to fine literary material.

4. May use teachers' manuals unbalanced with respect to reading skill development. These manuals may not provide sufficient direct or explicit explanations of comprehension skills and strategies for building background and may direct the teacher to ask too many comprehension questions following the reading of a story.

5. Uses workbook material that focuses on isolated skill development with little opportunity for integrating reading skills or applying comprehension-monitoring strategies.

Language Experience Approach

The language experience approach (LEA) is a language-arts approach to the teaching of reading using the child's own language. LEA presents reading as a natural extension of speaking. The most common activity is the dictation of a child's experiences to the teacher. The teacher writes down the child's story on a poster board (called an *experience chart*). These stories are then used to teach specific reading skills.

Advantages

1. Helps in explaining to children the relation of their oral language to written material.

2. Illustrates the close connection between what children say and what they will read.

3. Integrates the language arts into the elementary school curriculum.

4. Recognizes and respects a children's oral language in creating reading material.

5. Helps in showing children that reading is useful.

6. Provides high motivation to learn by using children's own language in creating reading material.

Disadvantages

1. If viewed as the total reading program, may limit children's exposure to fine literary material.

2. Provides no planned, sequential development of word-identification and comprehension skills and strategies.

3. Provides no planned, sequential development of reading vocabulary.

4. May limit children's understanding to their own written language, instead of opening them to what others have written.

Literature-Based Approach

The literature-based reading approach is a coordinated program using all types of literature as the catalyst in teaching children to read. Children are guided to an understanding, enjoyment, and appreciation of literature. Literature may supplement the basal reader and language experience approaches, or may be the primary source in teaching reading.

Advantages

1. Allows for the development and practice of language processes and strategies in quality literary material as opposed to sterile workbooks and other commercial kits and activities.

2. Promotes a joy of reading and an appreciation of all types of literature.

3. Uses literature as a means to improve reading vocabulary.

Disadvantages

If used as the core reading program:

1. Difficulty levels of some literature books may be problematic because of the wide range of reading ability within any grade level.

2. Teacher will need to supplement literary material with additional materials for practice of reading skills and strategies.

3. Has no planned, sequential, and explicit development of reading skills and strategies.

4. Basic skills as assessed on mandatory accountability tests may not be covered.

Whole Language Approach

The whole language approach is a language-arts approach closely related to the language experience and literature-based approaches. Based on the interdependent relationships of the language arts, classroom instruction focuses on developing both writing and reading in a natural way. Whole language programs stress practice activities in whole-text writing and reading, with little attention to direct instruction and practice of subskills, such as specific vowel sounds. Reading and writing are processes to be developed together, with daily journal writing a common procedure.

Advantages

1. Integrates reading with listening, speaking, and writing.

2. Fosters development of reading through whole texts rather than workbook activities.

3. Recognizes and respects children's oral and written language in creating reading material.

4. Encourages mutual development of reading and writing abilities.

5. Creates a desire to use and to refine language.

Disadvantages

1. Has no planned, sequential, and explicit development of word identification and comprehension skills and strategies.

2. Has no planned, sequential development of children's reading vocabulary.

3. If used as the core reading program, will need supplementing with literature and materials for practice and mastery of reading skills and strategies.

4. Basic skills as assessed on mandatory accountability tests may not be covered.

Principle 6: The effective reading teacher understands that students need to know a variety of ways to decode written language.   The ability to pronounce and interpret written symbols is an integral component of the reading process. However, identifying words is not reading but is a means for developing reading efficiency. Clearly, effective readers are superior in identifying words. The means to accomplish this component in the teaching of reading has been the subject of thousands of research studies. Unfortunately, the accumulated evidence has yielded no method successful with all children. Because of the unusual nature of our language (with its origins in several other languages) and differences among individual learners, the most sensible and successful approach to word identification is an eclectic one. Such an approach encourages students to develop a flexible, problem-solving attitude to identifying words by employing several means to decode them. By using varied methodologies, reading teachers can truly meet the varied needs of their students. The major approaches to decoding written language include: (1) learning words by sight without examining them carefully (sight vocabulary or whole word approach); (2) associating letters with the speech sounds they represent (phonics); (3) using the meaning of surrounding text (contextual analysis); and (4) utilizing the structural elements of a word (structural analysis).

The application of this principle of reading is directly related to comprehension. Once students have learned ways to automatically decode words (that is, to identify words quickly with minimal effort), they can devote more time to thinking about and reacting to ideas in text. In truth, good readers can make simultaneous use of the four approaches listed above to identify words on their own. The following paragraphs describe each of these word-identification strategies. Appendix D gives lists of sight vocabulary words recommended for use in teaching students, and Appendix E provides recommended lists of phonic generalizations.

Sight Vocabulary

Those words in our language that are irregular in nature (do not have a one-to-one sound/symbol relationship) can be learned through the sight vocabulary, or whole word, approach. In this approach (sometimes called the *sight word* or *look-say* approach), students learn a word by looking at it as a whole, not by dissecting it. Students must instantly recognize words learned by this methodology. Words are presented visually to students, pronounced by both teacher and students, discussed and used in sentences, and practiced independently by students. In almost every instance, words learned through the sight vocabulary approach need to be practiced in context in a variety of ways. The most common words taught by this approach include basic service words (for example, Johnson's basic vocabulary of sight words, presented in Appendix D), words of personal interest to students, words that appear regularly in students' first readers, and content-area words, such as geographical, scientific, and mathematical terms.

Phonics

Because English is an alphabetic language, letters represent speech sounds. However, our language has more speech sounds than letters to represent them, so that there is no consistent one-to-one sound/symbol relationship. Yet, phonics remains an important tool for students to use in identifying unknown words. Adams (1990-b) defines phonics as "a system of teaching reading that builds upon the alphabetic principle, [and one in] which a central component is the teaching of correspondences between letters or groups of letters and their pronunciations" (p. 12). To readily understand and apply sound/symbol relationships, students need to know automatically the consonant (whether single consonants, blends, or the clusters known as consonant digraphs) and vowel (long, short, and vowel digraphs) sounds and be able to blend word parts together rapidly. Especially for words that are regular in nature (have a one-to-one sound/symbol relationship), the application of phonic principles along with the context of the sentence will aid in decoding an unknown word.

Contextual Analysis

The third word identification strategy is the application of contextual clues. Contextual analysis involves teaching students to use semantics (in this case, the meaning of other words in a sentence and paragraph) to arrive at the pronunciation and meaning of an unknown word, and syntax (in this case, the arrangement of word order) to determine the word's part of speech and whether it is singular or plural. The conscious use of context will enable readers to arrive at the pronunciation and meaning of many words. Again, as is the case with the other strategies, contextual analysis (using both semantic and syntactic clue systems) is rarely used by itself but is best combined with phonics or structural analysis in decoding unknown words.

Structural Analysis

The fourth word-identification strategy focuses on meaningful structural units to help in decoding unknown words. In structural analysis, students identify a word's syllables, root element, prefixes, suffixes, compound elements, and inflectional endings to decode the whole. As with phonics, the use of structural analysis is dependent upon meaningful practice in context. It is also important to note that while syllabication is usually included under phonic analysis, it is technically a structural analysis skill, in which students apply vowel principles to pronounce a word.

Principle 7:   The effective reading teacher cultivates positive student attitudes and feelings.   A significant component of effective reading instruction is the pervasive emphasis on developing positive attitudes and feelings toward oneself and toward reading and learning. Years of observing successful classroom teachers and of studying the research literature on school- and teacher-effectiveness have reiterated our belief that increased student achievement goes hand in hand with positive student attitudes and feelings. Data also indicate a corresponding connection among students between difficulties in learning to read and low self-concepts and emotional stress. With the great importance placed on literacy in our society, it is no surprise to find that attaining that skill is a very stressful activity and that any difficulty encountered causes the emotional stress to increase (Gentile & McMillan, 1987). The reading process is sensitive to a variety of pressures from parents, peers, teachers, and other adults. (See Appendix I for the excellent list prepared by Gentile and McMillan (1984) to show threatening teacher practices that may create emotional conflict for students experiencing difficulties in reading.) By taking the following steps, classroom teachers of reading can help roll into one a concern for cognitive ends and, equally important, affective concerns:

- Recognize the importance that students' attitudes and feelings play in whether they are successful in learning to read.

- Know and capitalize upon students' interests and backgrounds in planning instruction.

- Plan a variety of reading activities in which all students will be successful; thus, as much as possible, attend to individual differences within a class.

- Monitor student feelings, involvement, and success in reading activities and provide timely feedback.

- Provide needed explanations and extra one-on-one instruction when students encounter difficulty.

- Communicate personal interest and friendliness to each student, stressing that he or she will be successful in the classroom this year.

- Be sensitive to students' verbal responses, looking for signs of confusion and lack of confidence, and to nonverbal cues, such as reactions to peers, facial expressions, and reactions to failure.

- Where possible, create a supportive, caring atmosphere by using cooperative grouping in which students can foster positive peer relationships.

Principle 8:   The effective reading teacher understands the role of assessing each student's strengths and weaknesses in providing successful instruction.   One of the major functions of reading teachers is to provide instruction based on students' needs. If teachers realize the relationship of assessment to instruction, they are aware of different means to determine specific strengths and weaknesses of their students. Effective assessment results in placing students at their appropriate instructional reading levels, determining appropriate teaching strategies based on the emotional and social needs of students, and identifying specific strong and weak areas in the processing of text information before, during, and after reading comprehension. In order to carry out an effective plan of assessment, teachers need to become familiar with and use a blend of formal and informal measures. The following is a sample list of such assessment measures:

- Interest inventory

- Checklists of reading behaviors

- Daily assignments

- Teacher-made tests

- Criterion-referenced tests

- Competency tests on basic skills;

- Standardized test results

- Informal Reading Inventory (IRI)

> • One-on-one interactions with students assessing specific text-processing strategies.

A balance of the more traditional tests and an informal one-on-one assessment of strategy use is desirable. A global view of a reading class in terms of levels of reading is important, but a more important point is the determination of specific strengths and weaknesses in the processes students employ to understand written ideas. Principle 16 presents more on gathering information about the processes students use and the importance of ongoing assessment. Effective instruction cannot begin until an assessment reveals specific areas of need. Once information is collected on students' reading behavior, teachers must synthesize this information and interpret the data in light of the overall goal of reading comprehension. Classroom teachers must interpret assessment information to know their students' range of ability, individual differences, and patterns of strengths and weaknesses. It is through collecting information from a variety of sources that teachers can formulate their prescriptive hunches or plans to guide their reading activities.

Principle 9: The effective reading teacher knows and applies specialized techniques when teaching students who speak a nonstandard dialect and students whose native language is not English. In today's schools, many students speak a dialect other than standard English and many are learning English as a second language. In both cases, to be successful, teachers of reading must know their students' backgrounds, must employ additional knowledge and skills in their teaching, and must use specialized techniques and guidelines in making instructional decisions in the classroom.

There are a number of dialects in the English language. According to Harris and Hodges (1981), a dialect is "a variety of the language of a speech community differing enough from other varieties of that language in pronunciation, grammar, and vocabulary to be considered a distinct type, but not a separate language because there is mutual understandability" (p. 87). Although standard English is most common in our country, there are dozens of dialects and it is important to realize that none is superior to the others, and that each is logical and governed by a set of internal rules. Furthermore, a student's competence is unrelated to his or her use of dialect. (See Appendix G for the characteristics of black English, a common dialect.) It is crucial that teachers be aware of dialects and know something about any dialects spoken by the students they teach. This is important for two reasons: First, by being aware of particular phonological, syntactical, and semantic differences, teachers will not count characteristics of the dialect as oral reading errors or miscues; second, teachers can show respect for a nonstandard dialect while at the same time modeling standard English. Awareness of dialectal errors that do or do not interfere with a reader's comprehension is also of importance. Without knowledge of a student's dialect, a teacher cannot make this determination and may falsely earmark a student for remediation. Specific instructional guidelines to use in planning and delivering effective instruction to students who speak a nonstandard dialect are:

- Become familiar with the dialect and note its specific differences from standard English.

- Do not penalize students for dialectal errors in reading as long as comprehension is unaffected.

- Respect and accept a student's dialect.

- Do not expect complete mastery of standard English before reading instruction can be initiated.

- Emphasize oral language development by exposure to literature.

- Model standard English through storytelling.

- Use the Language Experience Approach to teach reading initially and to illustrate to students that the goal of reading is understanding.

- Select materials to read that reflect students' backgrounds and interests.

- Design reading experiences so that students can be active and so there's much peer interaction.

In many of our schools, a large percentage of students have a native language other than English. It is not uncommon to have students whose native language is Polish, Navajo, Vietnamese, or Spanish, to name just a few. Hispanic students constitute a majority of non-English speakers in schools in the United States. (Appendix H contains a list of Spanish language features.) Since learning to read is a language process, it should be no surprise that many students whose native language is not English experience difficulties learning to read in English. Unlike students who speak a dialect, many of these students do not understand spoken English and know little written English. If students are orally fluent in English, the possible difficulties are not as great. To correct this language mismatch, schools sometimes employ English-as-a-Second-Language (ESL) and bilingual approaches. ESL focuses on teaching English orally to students who speak limited English before teaching them how to read. A school's ESL program is usually a *pull-out* (separate) class provided in addition to regular class instruction. Bilingual instruction is characterized by concurrently teaching reading in both the student's native language and English. Specific guidelines to use in planning and delivering instruction to students whose native language is not English are:

- Know the differences between standard English and the students' native language.

- Emphasize oral language activities to build students' listening and speaking vocabularies.

- Use the Language Experience Approach for beginning reading.

- Focus on the understanding of ideas, not correct pronunciation of words. Correct pronunciation is not the goal of reading instruction.

- Select materials to be read that reflect the students' background and cultural heritage.

This principle highlights again the diversity of students in our schools. This diversity is the one quality that makes teaching so rewarding. Teaching would be dull if all children were alike in all areas. With all children, especially those who speak a dialect other than standard English or whose native language is not English, teachers of reading must want to learn everything they can about their children and value the differences in them. Valuing and encouraging differences and realizing one has much to learn from all children and their backgrounds and culture are hallmarks of a true professional.

Principle 10:   The effective reading teacher utilizes a team approach to ensure that each student receives a sound educational program.   When we hear the often quoted expression, "The teacher is the single most significant factor in determining

Teachers who collaborate with other professionals are better able to provide meaningful reading instruction.
Barbara Schaudt

whether students will be successful in learning to read," it is easy to conclude that the teacher alone is responsible for excellence. However, such is not the case in today's reading program. Like professionals in all other fields, teachers of reading view themselves as part of a team, with many people to call on for help. Teachers working collectively with other interested people parallels the trend nationwide for teacher empowerment. Teachers are gaining increasing influence in educational decision-making. Learning the ability to work together, to give the best possible services to all children, is central to becoming a decision-maker. A solid foundation to meet individual needs of students necessitates a team approach. Because effective reading teachers recognize the importance of fostering their students' positive attitudes and feelings, as well as their cognitive growth, they gladly work with several different types of professionals, such as those listed below. Working closely and easily with these resource people and specialists, to provide the very best education for all students, is one characteristic of a true professional.

Parents. As their child's first teachers, parents are the source of invaluable information. They can provide insight on attitudes, feelings, interests, hobbies, talents, preferred learning styles, strengths, and weaknesses. Parents are partners in the educational process and can do much in the home to foster literacy.

Principal. As the curriculum leader of his or her school, a principal can provide excellent advice on contacting specialized help for certain students, obtaining specialized learning resources, and offering possible solutions to instructional dilemmas.

Guidance Counselors. With their primary concern being that of promoting students' physical, social, emotional, and educational well-being, guidance personnel are specialists who can aid classroom teachers with all their students, not only those with severe learning difficulties or behavior problems. These specialists can help teachers in recommending psychological approaches to teaching, giving direct help with individual children, and helping all students increase their self-esteem.

Social Worker. This specialist can provide invaluable aid to the classroom teacher by working directly with a child's parents concerning a school situation.

Special Education Teacher. This specialist can provide suggestions for mainstreaming handicapped children in the regular classroom and is a resource person for communicating with parents and other specialists.

Reading Specialist. This person is an excellent resource for specialized reading techniques and materials to use with children experiencing extreme difficulty in learning to read and for testing students who have serious reading problems.

Discussion Questions: Thinking About Planning Instruction

1. How is the development of oral language skills related to reading development? Can you cite specific examples from your classroom observations as illustrations?

2. How does planning differ for teaching basic skills and critical reading outcomes? Can you provide examples?

3. How does planning differ for students of differing ability levels? Can you provide examples?

4. Who makes the decision on what to teach at any given time?

5. What factors should influence how teachers plan their lessons?

6. Try to put yourself in the place of a frustrated reader in a classroom in which you are working at the moment. What do you feel? What do you need? What sensitivities should a teacher possess to meet your needs?

7. What affective and cognitive variables affect the learning of minority children in the classroom in which you are working? What are the students' motivational styles?

8. Do students need to learn how to identify unknown words all at once in the primary grades? Why or why not?

9. Many best-laid plans for an effective reading program go astray because of poor public relations and poor communication among classroom teachers, other school professionals, and parents. How can teachers strengthen public relations and communications?

10. React to the following statement: "Although it is important to project a positive attitude and have high expectations for students, it is equally important to realize that some students will never read at their projected grade level." Do you agree or disagree? Why?

Chapter

3

Principles 11–16:
Teaching Reading

Principle 11: The effective reading teacher knows the routine or procedure for teaching a story. Regardless of whether they are using a basal reader, a language experience story, or a literature story, effective teachers know the steps in teaching any form of text to students. The centerpiece of instruction—the main vehicle used to teach children to read—is the story. In fact, the primary overall goal of reading instruction is to foster independence in text-processing for students. Whether one is teaching vocabulary, presenting ways of decoding unknown words, providing comprehension strategies, suggesting study strategies, fostering reading as a leisure-time activity, exposing students to various forms of (and responses to) literature, or integrating reading with writing, the avenue used is some type of story or text. The procedure used to teach a story has been universal for years. A systematic procedure involving the steps of preparation for reading, actual reading, and review and development is recommended. This procedure is sometimes called the Directed Reading Activity (DRA) or the Directed Reading-Thinking Activity (DRTA), which focuses on prediction (Stauffer, 1975). The overall steps have remained the same, but modifications are needed to take into account recent research on how readers store, recall, and process information. The following plan shows the key components in teaching a story:

Preparation for Reading

- Discuss previous experiences related to the story.
- Present new information (building schema) necessary to understand the story.
- Develop interest in the story and motivation to read by relating the story to the students' own lives.
- Develop new vocabulary and concepts.
- Develop geographical setting if necessary.
- Teach new decoding or comprehension abilities to be used in the story.
- Review the organizational structure of the story.
- Set a purpose for reading and encourage students to predict events in the story.

Silent Reading

- Provide modeling before silent reading, and encourage students as they read silently to confirm their predictions, answer purpose-setting questions, reflect on ideas presented, slow their reading rate to understand ideas (or speed up when appropriate), and reread parts when appropriate.

Guided Follow-Up Activities

- Answer purpose-setting questions.
- Discuss outcome of pre-reading predictions.
- Reread portions of the story orally, having a specific purpose in mind.
- Summarize main ideas in the story.
- Develop understanding of the story at different cognitive levels by asking various comprehension questions.
- Combine reading and writing on topics related to the story.
- Practice new vocabulary and/or comprehension skills and strategies in a variety of formats and grouping plans.
- Complete extended or creative activities related to the story.

The watchword in using this universal routine is *flexibility*. There is no need to cover every single item listed above, nor is there a specific time allotment to give each component. Your exact routine will depend upon a host of factors, including the grade level, the needs and interests of your students, and your instructional goals. It is virtually impossible to complete all three components in one day. Because of the other activities involved in your reading/language arts classes, four or five days may be needed to effectively cover all aspects of a story. Also, unless the teacher is trying to promote literature for its own worth and enjoyment, a story is only the means to an end. In this sense, a story is a vehicle to teach students to better comprehend what they read.

Each teacher should deviate from the above routine depending on students' reactions, creative responses, or lack of understanding of a particular point. Each teacher must keep his or her goals foremost in mind, but remain sensitive to students' needs and modify the routine accordingly. Using this routine in a lock-step fashion for every story is certain to result in intolerable boredom for both students and teachers.

Principle 12: The effective reading teacher uses the direct, or explicit, model of instruction for teaching specific reading skills, abilities, and strategies. The most pervasive conclusion of teacher effectiveness studies from the early 1970s was that teachers have a profound influence on how much students learn. Implicit in this conclusion is the corollary that effective teachers use a variety of instructional methods depending upon their goal. For those reading skills and abilities that are specific in nature (for example, auditory and visual discrimination, decoding abilities, reading vocabulary development, sequential development of ideas, cause-and-effect relationships, fact and opinion, identification of main ideas, and a summarization ability), one effective approach focuses on the teacher directly explaining the new skill or ability in small steps, coupled with supervised practice and an abundance of independent practice in real reading situations. Teacher-supervised and independent practice can be accomplished in a variety of settings, especially in cooperative learning groups. (Appendix F presents the specific steps in this approach.) In this approach, the teacher clearly leads the teaching-learning process. Students are more likely to pay attention, and thus learn more. This teaching approach is certainly not new, but is supported in the recent literature on effective teaching. The approach brings together many recommended components of effective instruction and of schema theory, including relating new information to past learning, explaining to students why the new skill or ability is important and useful, eliciting student interest, providing step-by-step explanation and examples, summarizing main points, providing supervised or guided practice, and practicing the new ability in a variety of reading texts and groupings. In effect, this approach embodies the old saying, "Tell them what you are going to tell them; then tell them; then tell them what you told them." As with any teaching method, this approach is not successful with all types of objectives and can be misused. Each step in this approach should be modified to meet student needs and the topic at hand. If the direct or explicit model of instruction is a part of the reading teacher's repertoire of teaching methods, students are more likely to learn essential reading skills and abilities.

Principle 13:   The effective reading teacher designs specific learning experiences to promote critical thinking through reading and writing.   With the shift to viewing reading as an active, problem-solving process, the topic of critical thinking as a goal in reading instruction has received renewed attention. In today's world, literacy involves much more than merely comprehending ideas on a literal level. It includes the ability to thoughtfully assess, analyze, and evaluate ideas and arguments. The critical reader is a reflective thinker, who responds with healthy skepticism to the text and in effect asks, "So what?"

Critical thinking doesn't develop by chance. Teachers of reading can promote critical thinking in their students by:

- Being critical readers themselves and sharing this excitement with students.

- Asking questions of students that require higher cognitive-level processing.

- Allocating sufficient class time to promote critical thinking.

- Designing lessons and activities specifically aimed at promoting critical thinking.

First, unless the teacher understands critical thinking and *is* a critical thinker, it is unlikely that his or her students will develop these abilities. The teacher must read critically and

Effective teachers devote considerable time to designing learning experiences that will improve their students' critical-thinking abilities.
Barbara Schaudt

share reading experiences with the students. Second, while it is certainly easier to ask low cognitive-level questions during discussions of stories, it is much more exciting and beneficial to students if they are routinely asked high-level questions. Teachers should strive for a balance between low- and high-level questions during discussion periods. If students are not asked to think critically about what they read, they will simply not do so. Third, allocation of time is crucial to developing critical thinking. Students cannot be expected to develop into critical, reflective readers without the opportunity to do so. However, while time itself is important, what the teacher does with that time is even more important. Thus the fourth way to promote critical thinking is to systematically plan learning experiences that require critical thinking.

When the goal of instruction is the learning of a specific skill or ability, the direct or explicit approach is appropriate, with the teacher being in direct control of the class at all times. In fostering critical thinking, a different approach is required: The teacher should act more as a facilitator than a director in exposing students to assignments requiring critical analysis. In this approach, the students are more active in the learning process and have more input in the lesson activity. (Note, however, that the teacher must expect more movement and noise in the classroom as a result.) Critical thinking assignments can be a vital way for students to apply their reading abilities. In such activities, students collect, organize, and criticize information on a topic of interest to them. In doing so, they must classify, interpret, and react critically to the information they read. A complete listing of thinking activities for all grade levels is found in the excellent book by Raths, Wassermann, Jonas, and Rothstein (1986). Sample topics of creative assignments, which may be done individually or as group projects, might include how man studies the weather; the Persian Gulf War; music of the 1970s; the lives and accomplishments of prominent Americans, such as President John Kennedy, Gen. Colin Powell, Martin Luther King, Jr., Sandra Day O'Connor, Interior Secretary Manuel Lujan, and astronaut Sally Ride; capital punishment; oil and the Middle East; China today; nuclear vs. solar energy; changes in Eastern Europe and the Soviet Union; Egypt; and life in our city fifty years ago.

An immense variety of books and printed material of all kinds is available for today's reading program. The vehicles to promote critical thinking have increased with the advent of more literature-based reading in schools. Gentile and McMillan (1989) recommend placing greater emphasis on literature to promote higher-order thinking, especially with "at-risk" students. Their compelling rationale for using fine literary material is presented below.

> Literature is the vehicle for helping "at-risk" students make sense out of and through written language. It provides them the means to apply skills contextually using rich material that educates and entertains. Moreover, good literature is knowledge-based and furnishes these students a broad range of historical, geographical, political, scientific, mathematic, religious, biological and literary information. It stirs wonderment and imagination, facilitates these students' understanding of themselves and others and the world they live in, and offers them a sense of identity or control that can empower the spirit and motivate them to express their thoughts and feelings (p. 12).

Although much of the class time devoted to critical thinking assignments will be spent in students working alone or in small cooperative groups, teachers must be explicit in their initial explanation of critical thinking ability, and be able to model its implementation to students. In this way, students initially learn critical thinking skills and abilities through a variation of the direct instruction approach. Teachers need to access students' knowledge and experiences, and then explain, model, and "think aloud" various skills and abilities. In addition, students should be allowed independent time with few restrictions to develop these critical thinking abilities around a literature base.

Principle 14:   The effective reading teacher teaches content-reading skills and studying strategies so that students will be able to remember, organize, and retrieve information from expository text.   Success in the regular reading program does not automatically spell success in reading for content. Naturally, there is much carryover into content reading of skills and strategies used in the regular reading program. However, there are significant differences. Most stories students read during reading instruction are written in narrative form, whereas content material is written in an expository structure. Expository text lies at a higher readability or difficulty level because of the large number of concepts presented, and difficult vocabulary is presented in a different organizational pattern. (See the capsule summary of expository text structures in Appendix A.) Expository text is also characterized by its compact presentation of information. The teaching procedure for content materials is a modification of the Directed Reading Activity or Directed Reading-Thinking Activity. Viewing reading as a problem-solving activity, teachers should use a procedure similar to that described in Principle 11.

Success in understanding any new content requires readers to learn and apply specific skills needed in each subject—and to learn and use specific studying and metacognitive strategies—before, during, and after reading content material. In addition, students need to be able to apply these abilities to everyday, functional reading tasks: reading a newspaper, a menu, a telephone directory, a road map, and so forth. The following skills are required in each subject and must be directly taught to students:

In Math, the ability to:

1. Use a slow and deliberate reading rate.

2. Master technical vocabulary and symbols.

3. Follow directions.

4. Apply learned concepts to new situations.

In Social Studies, the ability to:

1. Follow ideas and events in sequence.

2. Read maps, tables, time lines, and graphs.

3. Outline main ideas.

4. Follow directions.

5. Master a specialized vocabulary.

6. Use reference materials.

In Science, the ability to:

1. Follow sequence.

2. Follow directions.

3. Classify details and main ideas.

4. Interpret graphic material visually.

5. Apply learned concepts to new situations.

6. Master a specialized vocabulary.

A second major area in content reading is the application of metacognitive and studying strategies for successful comprehension. *Metacognition* in reading is the reader's ability to be aware of and control his or her reading behavior. To comprehend content material, students must learn and strategically apply various studying strategies before, during, and after reading. Successful readers establish purposes for themselves to complete a task. Purposes provide a reason for reading. By explicitly teaching the following skills and strategies, and by modeling and thinking aloud the thinking process used to make sense of text, teachers can better equip their students to comprehend content material. Students should:

Before Reading

• Possess the reading skills (listed above) needed in each content area.

• Detect the author's pattern or organizational structure.

• Read the introduction.

• Examine all visual aids throughout the chapter—pictures, maps, graphs, diagrams, and so forth.

• Learn key vocabulary.

- Predict what will be discussed.

- Review his or her knowledge of the topic and relate it to the material to be read.

- Read each chapter summary.

- Read questions at the end of each chapter.

- Set purposes to direct his or her reading.

During Reading

- Turn each item in bold print into a question, and read to find the answer.

- Use various checking strategies—reread to understand a point, summarize a difficult idea, make notes in margins, hypothesize about what will happen next, question one-self about the meaning of key vocabulary and main ideas, highlight main points in the text, answer some of his or her purpose-setting questions.

After Reading

- Answer purpose-setting questions.

- Verify or reject hypotheses.

- Answer end-of-chapter questions.

- Summarize main ideas.

- Reread parts of a chapter for comprehension breakdown.

Principle 15:   The effective reading teacher recognizes the importance of, and promotes, recreational reading.   The ultimate goal of teaching reading is to produce independent, critical, and flexible readers who *like* to read. This goal is highly prized in our society. All the best intentions and instructions are lost if students cannot apply their abilities in new situations and do not choose to read on their own. Opening up students to the world through good literature, magazines, and newspapers should be a primary goal of reading instruction at every grade level. However, this goal must be systematically planned for and developed. Students will learn to value reading as both a functional and a leisure-time activity given the proper guidance by classroom teachers. Teachers can "make good" on this all-important goal of fostering a love of reading by: (1) reading good stories and books aloud to students;

Students and teachers read literature together and share with one another their insights and feelings.
Stuart Spates

(2) setting aside 15 to 30 minutes each day for students to silently read material of their own choice (an activity called Uninterrupted Sustained Silent Reading, or USSR; see Hunt, 1970); (3) book-selling sessions and reading plays or acting out favorite parts or characters from books; (4) creating interest groups around particular topics or books; (5) capitalizing on students' interests by carefully selecting the reading materials used for instructional purposes; (6) encouraging wide reading by making a "reading corner" or "reading center" in the classroom; (7) encouraging students to use their town library by keeping them abreast of library happenings; (8) encouraging reading at home by explaining to parents the benefits of reading to their children; and (9) periodically inviting a storyteller to your classroom, or telling stories to your students yourself. An excellent source for other practical ideas on developing a successful recreational-reading program is the paperback by Spiegel (1981).

Wide reading also helps students to reinforce and extend their existing skills and strategies. Students are taught reading abilities and strategies in the instructional program, but these same skills and strategies are then practiced in independent or recreational reading. Students need interesting and varied reading for their abilities to become automatic. For example, the ability to identify new words automatically allows students to devote more attention to deriving meaning from the text. This argument is cyclical, for without abundant practice and automatic text-processing, chances are slim that students will desire to read on their own. Furthermore, wide reading is a primary means of enlarging one's vocabulary. Research by Nagy and Herman (1987) indicates that increases in student vocabularies result from increased recreational reading outside the classroom.

Principle 16: The effective reading teacher knows the importance of continuously assessing students during instruction and of adjusting some students' programs after gathering new information. The evaluation of learning objectives at the end of a book, a unit, or a school term is certainly a crucial aspect of instruction. Equally crucial is the day-by-day, ongoing assessment of students' reading skills and strategies. It is extremely difficult, if not impossible, to initiate any meaningful reading instruction without first assessing a student's instructional reading level and his or her specific strengths and weaknesses in deriving meaning from text. Once this assessment is made, an initial plan of instruction can be devised and acted upon. Yet, this initial assessment should not be the final word. Indeed, subsequent instruction should be used to confirm the assessment, reject it entirely, or adjust it, based on student performance.

An analogy may be drawn between the teacher and the family doctor. When you go to your doctor with stomach pains, the doctor studies your medical history and examines you. If your condition does not improve with treatment, further tests may be suggested or a new treatment prescribed. Similarly, after collecting relevant data on a youngster, the teacher prescribes a program. However, if the student does not progress, a change in the program is warranted. Such a program demands continuous assessment—not just initial screening in September.

If a teacher realizes that students have individual interests, abilities, and rates of learning, and that all these change, it follows that his or her assessment should continue at all times. This means that instructional goals, classroom activities, and teaching materials are continually reshaped to meet student need. For example, instruction in metacognitive strategies to use before, during, and after reading may be based on some informal or formal assessment. However, the sequence, classroom activities, and materials used may change constantly depending on students' interest, area of learning, and the type of instruction.

For students to grow in their reading abilities, teachers need to custom-tailor, or personalize, the learning experience. This type of instruction is specific in nature and tied directly to how a student derives meaning from text. While periodic formal testing can help in assessment, informal, one-on-one interactions with students are most productive and beneficial activities. Such interaction is called process-oriented assessment. It focuses on determining strengths and weaknesses in the strategies a student uses in comprehending text. It involves asking the student to summarize and react to specific questions on how he or she prepares to read, the techniques used while reading, and postreading strategies used to make sure he or she understood what was read. This assessment relies on the manner in which student and teacher interact where both can gain insights into strengths of, and impediments to, the comprehension process. Whether a student reads a portion of a text aloud or silently, or takes part in a group assignment, the adept teacher knows what to look for and what to ask students to gauge his or her ability to comprehend text successfully. Here are some questions to ask students themselves, or to infer from student performance. Does the student:

Generally

- show facility in identifying words?
- apply word identification strategies in context?
- understand the meaning of key vocabulary terms?

Before Reading

- establish purposes for reading?
- relate what will be read to experience?
- predict what will happen in the text?
- identify the author's pattern of developing ideas?

During Reading

- use various comprehension strategies, such as stopping to understand a point, verifying an initial prediction and initiating a new prediction, rereading a portion of text to aid comprehension, and inferring a main idea?

After Reading

- determine what is most important to remember?

- summarize main ideas?

- answer purpose-setting questions and verify initial pre-dictions?

By pooling this information, the teacher can determine priorities for instruction. This filtering process directly responds to students' ability to process meaning. In this way, students' programs can be tailored to suit their individual needs. This ongoing, process-oriented assessment also gives students a clearer understanding of their own reading strategies and what their teachers expect them to learn. Wittrock (1987) states that process-oriented measures of comprehension

> will not tell what your students have learned about a text passage. Nor will they tell you where your students' reading achievement lies in relation to the strategies your students use to make sense out of the text they read in your class. They will provide a way for you to understand the instruction in comprehension your students need. They will tie teaching problems closely to the research literature on how to teach comprehension strategies. (p. 736)

Discussion Questions: Thinking About Teaching Reading

1. From your perspective, what forces work against providing all students with the best possible instruction?

2. What are some examples of prereading literary experiences for children?

3. How can the backgrounds of culturally and linguistically diverse children be capitalized upon in a reading lesson? Can you give a specific example of how you would use their background? Why is it important to be aware of cultural differences when working with children?

4. What are the advantages of presenting students with a clear-cut assessment of their reading strengths and weaknesses? Are there disadvantages to doing so?

5. How can teachers extend students' interests?

6. How can teachers show students that reading can be exciting? Can you provide examples?

7. How much time should be devoted to silent reading? Reading aloud? Will the ratio be different for various grade levels? Why or why not?

8. What are some alternatives to the standard book report that will motivate students to share their experiences with literature?

9. What types of strategies and activities can a teacher use in teaching reading lessons around different forms of literature?

10. Can literature be used effectively with "at-risk" children? How?

11. Can literature be used to teach critical thinking? If so, how?

12. Why is it that a student's general reading ability does not predict how well he or she will be able to read for content?

13. From your interactions with elementary students, do you feel that most like to read on their own? What factors do you feel influence whether a student will want to read on his or her own?

Chapter 4

Principles 17–18: Managing and Organizing the Classroom

Principle 17: The effective reading teacher uses a variety of grouping procedures to help students learn. Years ago, because of the large number of students in a class, grouping was thought a necessary evil. Today the literature on effective teaching tells us that grouping for instruction is a means to capitalize on student differences and increase student achievement. Students learn from one another in a group, and are more likely to work productively in groups than individually. (This assumes that there are twenty to thirty, not five to ten, students in the classroom.) Different types of groupings include the following: whole, small, partner, and individual groups, based in turn on reading ability, interest, research, and cooperative learning. Effective teachers use a variety of groupings throughout the year to fit specific tasks. In this way, grouping is an integral part of providing individualized or personalized instruction. Each type of group is listed with the assumptions underlying its use.

Whole Group	Appropriate when all members of the class need a particular skill or strategy.
Small Group	Based on need; appropriate when a diagnosis reveals a certain number of students need the same skill or strategy.

Partner Group	Appropriate when two students can learn and practice a reading skill or strategy together.
Individual	Appropriate for individual children needing a particular skill or strategy.
Ability Group	Appropriate at times, but to be used with great caution for students of similar ability needing instruction at a particular reading level.
Interest Group	Appropriate for a variety of reading and language arts activities; students who share a common interest are grouped together.
Research Group	Appropriate for students completing a research activity together.
Cooperative Group	Appropriate for students learning and practicing a reading skill or strategy or completing a creative project together.

Special care must be exercised in using ability and cooperative groupings. Although ability grouping helpfully narrows the range of ability a teacher has to deal with in a class, the possible negative effects often outweigh this initial potential advantage. Negative practices sometimes associated with ability grouping include the teacher's inadvertently treating groups differently according to whether they are labelled of high, middle, or low ability; that is, the teacher may give more time, attention, smiles, physical contact, comprehension instruction, wait-time, and higher cognitive-level questions to high-ability groups. Those placed in low-ability reading groups may suffer lowered views of themselves. Also, without continuous diagnosis, many low-group students remain in the low group throughout their school careers. If grouping by ability is used, it is wise to employ other types of grouping as well. It is crucial that teachers be aware of the possible negative effects of ability grouping and guard against them to ensure each student a quality education.

Cooperative grouping is becoming enormously popular, and justifiably so. Research on teaching and learning supports the use of cooperative grouping at all grade levels. Cooperative

An important job in managing and organizing the classroom is monitoring students' progress in their seatwork activities.
Stuart Spates

grouping can be an alternative to ability grouping during the reading period. In cooperative groups, the teacher assigns students of varying academic abilities to work together on an activity. Although cooperative grouping takes different forms, one common procedure is to first give all students an explicit explanation of a skill or strategy, and then form cooperative groups of students of varying abilities (low, middle, and high) to work together on supervised and independent activities. Students are encouraged to help one another; they then receive a *group* evaluation or grade upon completion of the activity. Crucial to the success of cooperative grouping is the teacher's step-by-step modeling and guidance to students in how to conduct interpersonal relations and small group interactions; the teacher must also monitor each group's effectiveness. The objective in cooperative grouping is to communicate to the students that they can achieve their goal only by working with the other students within their group. This cooperative-goal structure is quite different from the competitive-goal structure, which implies that students can achieve a goal only if other students seeking the same goal fail. Cooperative grouping fosters greater peer interaction and learning, and creates a team feeling among students. It is important to note that research indicates students of all abilities, especially the low-ability students, benefit from this type of grouping.

Principle 18: The effective reading teacher exercises efficient management techniques to capitalize on time allocated for instruction. Teachers at all levels quickly realize the importance of being able to manage simultaneously the curriculum, the classroom environment, and their students in the most efficient manner possible to promote learning. The effective teacher of reading must first be knowledgeable about the reading process, approaches, materials, diagnostic procedures, and the rest of the content listed in the previous principles of instruction. If the average class comprised only three to six students, management would still be a concern, but one of only secondary importance. However, classroom teachers of reading must design and implement instruction for classes holding twenty to thirty students. (And, of course, teachers have no input into or choice about who will be assigned to their classes.)

There are no sure-fire recipes or universal prescriptions for efficient classroom management in all situations. Effective management is influenced by many factors—individual differences in students, instructional goals, materials, grouping procedures, and grade level, to name a few. However, one distinguishing characteristic of all effective manager-teachers is that they spend much time and effort *before* they teach, planning for meaningful experiences (Good & Brophy, 1987). The following are other important guidelines for making management decisions:

- Be yourself. Effective managers come in all personalities.

- Discuss class rules and your expectations for good behavior with students at the beginning of the year. With primary-grade students, model appropriate ways of completing basic tasks.

- Walk through your reading routines and lessons before teaching. Successful managers know their material, rehearse how each lesson will proceed, have established fall-back routines in case students do not finish an activity (or finish it early), know how to handle the transition from one group to the next, know how to handle seatwork activities, and are prepared to handle minor disruptions.

- Use a variety of materials, grouping arrangements, and creative activities to foster student interest in learning.

- Monitor students' progress in their seatwork activities.

- Be enthusiastic in your teaching. You are giving your students a gift; your enthusiasm will positively affect your students' attitude toward reading.

- Give praise to students for *specific* accomplishments. Avoid the habit of continually giving general praise to your students.

- Be alert for signs of confusion, difficulty, and boredom, and change the pace of your lesson accordingly.

- If discipline problems occur, stay calm, and avoid an extreme reaction, such as shouting or using sarcasm. Remind misbehaving students of your expectations for proper behavior.

**Discussion
Questions:
Thinking
About
Managing
and
Organizing
the
Classroom**

1. How can a teacher personalize instruction in a group setting?

2. What are the four or five most common management or discipline problems found in the reading class? Can you think of two or three possible solutions to each problem? Which solutions are most appropriate? Why?

3. One major problem teachers have is maintaining student engagement in reading activities while working with another group of students. What are some possible solutions to this dilemma?

4. What are the possible negative effects of overemphasizing a concern for: Student attitudes? Classroom discipline? Covering a certain amount of material in a limited amount of time? Basic skill mastery?

5. Discovering the correct pace for a lesson is crucial to successful teaching. How is this discovery made?

Model Lesson Plans

Part III

In this section of the text, fifteen model lesson plans are presented to help you design your own plans for teaching reading. The lessons represent a variety of major teaching strategies to teach reading in today's classroom. Most important, they represent major activities effective teachers use in the teaching of reading. When a layperson, administrator, or school board member asks the question, "Exactly what are the major teaching functions or performance expectations of a teacher of reading?" a listing of the major types of lessons and routines is necessary to answer the question. The following lesson plans span different reading approaches, all grade levels, essential elements of the reading process, and phases of a total reading program. Most of the lesson plans in this section include similar components. The components and a brief description of each are provided below:

Instructional Objective	The goal of the lesson.
Readiness	The manner in which the teacher motivates the students, develops the background of the lesson, and communicates the purpose of the lesson to students.
Step-By-Step Explanation	The manner in which the teacher explains or demonstrates the new strategy or skill to students.

Guided Practice	A practice activity on the new strategy or skill completed by the students and teacher together.
Independent Practice	A practice activity on the new strategy or skill completed by students independently.
Extension Activity	Further practice to help ensure the transfer of the strategy or skill to other types of activities.

Chapter 5

The Model Lesson Plans—and Their Effective Use

Any lesson plan or routine must be modified to meet the individual needs of students. Still, it is crucial that apprentice reading teachers not only know the major teaching functions, but also be able to plan and carry out lessons and routines in those areas. Each lesson plan is a blueprint for accomplishing instructional goals. Just as good readers are active in their search for meaning, the good reading teacher is active in planning and following through with a lesson. Effective teachers reflect on their teaching and modify future lessons based on student responses. The following are some of the essential questions a reading teacher should ask himself or herself when implementing any lesson or routine.

Before Teaching

- What prerequisite knowledge and skills do my students need to be successful with the present lesson?

- At what pace do I want to conduct the lesson? What will be the most troublesome areas for my students?

- How will I tie the objective of the lesson to previous learning of my students?

During Teaching

- Do my students understand the lesson objective?

- Do my students need additional explanation and practice?

After Teaching

- Do I need to reteach a part of the lesson?
- What did I learn today that will be of help in tomorrow's lesson?
- What are my reflections on the lesson?

As stated, the following lessons represent the major teaching functions in teaching reading. These functions or areas considered essential to teacher performance are:

- Emergent literacy
- Using a language experience approach
- The reading-writing connection: using predictable literature
- Teaching a literature-based basal story

Shared lessons and routines have built-in opportunities for children to read and write using fine literary material.
Stuart Spates

- **Word identification**

- **Comprehension**

- **Strategic reading**

- **Vocabulary**

- **Functional reading**

- **Integrated reading-language arts unit**

In your practicum experiences, it is important to plan and teach lessons in as many of these areas as possible. It is hoped that you will use these lessons as examples in designing your own. There is no simple recipe for each lesson —you must try one way, assess its effectiveness, and modify your next lesson to fit each unique situation. (Appendix J provides several blank lesson-plan forms.) The teaching of reading spans a variety of learnings. Therefore, some of the lessons have specific objectives, while others are designed to foster critical thinking. When the lesson goal is quite specific, the lesson itself will be more direct, with clearly distinguishable step-by-step procedures. If the lesson goal is teaching a critical thinking ability, a more indirect procedure with less teacher control is warranted. In addition, the more inclusive strategies of teaching a story (directed reading activity), using a language experience approach, or using predictable books with students all require different styles of interacting with students. Finally, as you design and teach various lessons, it is crucial that you continuously reflect on your actions, monitor your effectiveness, and evaluate your lessons. It is in this way you will grow in your ability and confidence to teach reading.

Emergent Literacy

Instructional Objective

Given magazine advertisements and instruction, the students will be able to communicate their thoughts in writing.

Readiness

We have been learning to write words using the best spelling we can. You already know that when you write it's okay if the words are not spelled perfectly. Right now we are working on ideas; later we can fix our spelling. We have also been learning that the words we speak can be written down. Today I'm going to give you pictures from magazines. The pictures are of things we buy. Then I'm going to ask you to tell me about the picture. After that, you'll write what you told me and draw a picture to match. If you understand that written words have meaning and make sense, you'll be better able to read.

Step-By-Step Explanation

(Show a McDonald's advertisement.) Look at this picture. Let's talk about McDonald's. Tell me everything that you know about McDonald's. (Record on the board what the students say, maintaining the integrity of the students' language. Pronounce each word as you write it. Read each sentence or thought using a natural rhythm and a natural voice. Be sure to accept single words and phrases. If necessary, ask questions such as, "What can we buy at McDonald's? When you go to McDonald's, what do you like to get? What foods are on a Big Mac? How do we get the food at McDonald's? Does a waiter or waitress bring the food to us?") When we write, we tell about the things we know, don't we?

Guided Practice

(Provide a set of selected advertisements.) This time I'd like you to choose your own picture. Pick one you know so that it will be easier to write about. Think about the picture and then write what you think, using your best spelling. After you've finished writing, read to me what you've written. Then you can draw your picture to match.

Independent Practice

Now each of you can have your own magazine. Look through the magazine and find any picture you like. Remember to choose a magazine that has a picture of something you know. Next, tear out the picture. These are old magazines and I'm giving you permission, so it's okay to tear out the picture. Then I'd like you to write what you know about the picture. After you finish writing, you can draw a picture to match what you wrote. When we are all through with this activity, we will read to each other what we wrote.

Extension Activities

Direct the children to bring labels of products from home. Have them write about their product. Encourage them to read to the class what they have written.

Ask the children to draw pictures of their favorite activities, people, pets, and so forth, using one page for each. Have them write about their pictures. Bind each child's pictures with a construction-paper cover. Encourage the students to read their "book" to the class.

Using a Language
Experience Approach:
An Experience Chart

Instructional Objective

Given the stimulus of a marine hermit crab and discussion about it, the student will be able to dictate and read sentences about the hermit crab.

Readiness

We have been learning that the words we speak can be written down, and that the print you see in books uses some of the same words we use when we talk. Today we are going to look at a special animal called a marine hermit crab. After we look at the crab, touch it, and talk about it, you are going to tell me about what you saw and what you learned. I'll write down what you say. Then we can read what you told me. You will be better able to read this story because all the words will be your very own.

Step-By-Step Explanation

Let's look at the marine hermit crab. Marine hermit crabs are very shy. They will come part of the way out of their shells if you are very quiet. Loud noises scare them and they will hide in their shells, so you need to be very quiet. After they are here for a little while, in a quiet place, we can make a loud noise and see what happens. What you need to do right now is be very quiet and look closely at the marine hermit crab, then tell me what you notice about it. (If necessary, encourage discussion by asking questions.) Let's look at its legs. Those things on the end of its legs are called pincers. How many legs does it have? Are all the legs and pincers the same size? Which ones seem to be bigger? Which are smaller? When it walks, which way does it move? (Take the crab out of its container, allow it to move about on the floor, and discuss its movement.) Where are its eyes? Where are its ears? Does it have any ears? What colors are its shell? What do you think the hermit crab might eat? How can we find out? (Throughout the lesson, refer to elementary reference books to determine the answers to the questions with the students.) The shell is not part of the marine hermit crab's body. Marine hermit crabs have to find a shell to live in. Where might they find their shells? What do you think the marine hermit crab has to do to take its shell with it? When do you think it might leave its shell? We already know the shell is not a part of the crab's body. We also already learned what marine hermit crabs like to eat. What happens over a long time when animals get older and keep eating? So, when do you think a marine hermit crab might leave its shell? (Continue to use the reference books to answer the questions if necessary.) Now when I say "Go," let's all make a loud noise by clapping and see what happens. When I say "Stop," you need to stop clapping. "Go!" "Stop!" What happened when we clapped?

Guided Practice

Now we are ready to write about what we learned and what we saw. What did we look at today? That's right; a marine hermit crab. Let's call our story "Marine Hermit Crabs." (Write the title of the story on large chart paper.) Who can tell me what the marine hermit crab looks like? (Guide the direction of the story so it has coherence by asking students to describe specific aspects of the crab. As students tell what it looks like, record their sentences on the chart paper, maintaining the integrity of the students' language. Pronounce each word as you write it. Read the sentence back using a natural rhythm and a natural voice. Have the students read each sentence together.)

Independent Practice

This time I'd like you to go back to your seats and take out a sheet of paper. Draw a picture of the marine hermit crab. Then write a sentence about what you liked best about the marine hermit crab. If you need help, I'll write your sentence for you. When you're done, I'll ask you to read to me the sentence you wrote.

Extension Activities

Ask the students what else they would like to know about the marine hermit crab. Take them to the library to find simple reference books that might address their interests.

Use the story on a daily basis so the students can reinforce reading their own words.

Use the story to teach a skill, such as beginning consonant sounds.

The Reading-Writing Connection: Using Predictable Literature

Instructional Objective

After listening to a reading aloud of *Brown Bear, Brown Bear, What Do You See?*, by Bill Martin, Jr.,* the student will be able to write predictable text based on the model.

Readiness

We have been learning about becoming authors and how to write sentences. We have also been learning that the words in books have to make sense. You already know that good readers try to guess what the author is going to say next. Remember that the words and the pictures can help us make good guesses about what the author will say next. If you can think about what the author is saying, the stories you read will make more sense.

Step-By-Step Explanation

Listen while I start reading *Brown Bear, Brown Bear, What Do You See?*, by Bill Martin, Jr., to you. After I have read a few pages, I am going to ask you to guess what you think the author will say next. (Read the first four pages or as many as necessary until you think the students understand the text pattern.

* Martin, B., Jr. (1983). *Brown Bear, Brown Bear, What Do You See?* New York: Holt, Rinehart and Winston.

Show the "yellow duck" page.) What do you think the author will ask on this page? ("Yellow duck, yellow duck, What do you see?") The yellow duck answers, "I see a blue horse looking at me." (Show the "blue horse" page.) What do you think the words on the next page will say? ("Blue horse, blue horse, What do you see?") The blue horse answers, "I see a green frog looking at me." (Continue to the end of the book.)

Guided Practice

Let's read the first two pages of *Brown Bear* again. This time we'll begin making our own book, using *Brown Bear* as an example to follow. I'd like you to think of an animal you like and a color you like. (Call on a student to tell you his or her animal and color. Incorporate the student's choice into the pattern. For example, "Gray elephant, gray elephant, What do you see?") What would you like the gray elephant to see? (Write the student's response. For example, "I see an orange rhino looking at me." Continue this pattern for each student on a separate piece of paper.) Now we can draw pictures to match our words. What picture will you draw to go with the words, "Gray elephant, gray elephant, What do you see?" What picture will you draw to go with the words, "I see an orange rhino looking at me"?

Independent Practice

Now you can go back to your seats and write more pages for your book. (Be certain to accept invented spellings.) After you write your sentences, draw pictures to match. When you have finished, you can bring your pages to me and we'll staple them together with a cover. Then you can read what you've written to me. Later in the day when we have "Author of the Day" time, you can share your story by reading it to an audience, our class.

Extension Activities

Have the students read their books to other classes.

Use the same exercise to teach adjectives.

Use predictable literature, such as *The Jolly Postman, or, Other People's Letters*, by Jan and Janet Allsberg, with older students.

Direct older students to read Beverly Cleary's *Dear Mr. Henshaw* and have them write letters to famous individuals.

Encourage your students to use computer telecommunications to write to other students from different communities or different states.

Teaching a
Literature-Based
Basal Story

The following is a teaching plan for the Level 5 (end of first grade) basal story from Harcourt Brace Jovanovich's Reading Program. Most basal programs today incorporate the interactive features of the reading process (building on knowledge, setting purposes and predicting, confirming predictions, and summarizing key ideas), and integrate the language arts around a literature base. Even with newer and improved basal programs, the classroom teacher remains the key ingredient in whether children are successful. Effective teachers view basal lesson plans for individual stories as suggestions, not directives. *Effective teachers pick, choose, and modify appropriate strategies from each basal lesson plan to fit their children's learning needs.* You are encouraged to "walk through" this basal lesson plan by first skimming the various sections to comprehend major components and their interrelatedness, then studying each section carefully to gain a clearer understanding of how to teach various reading strategies and skills through a story format.

Daisy's Surprise

by Dolly Cebulash

PAGES 166–175

The Lesson at a Glance	Core	As Needed
1 **PREPARING FOR READING**		
Lesson Vocabulary	●	
R¹ Initial /str/str		●
R³, T Initial /st/st		
R¹ Draw Conclusions (Applied in Step 2)		●
2 **READING AND RESPONDING TO THE SELECTION**		
Read and Discuss the Selection	●	
INTEGRATING THE LANGUAGE ARTS		
Think & Write: Write a Thank-you Note		●
Vocabulary: Synonyms, Antonyms, and Comparatives		●
Oral Reading: Establish Mood		●
Reading Across the Curriculum (Language, Art)		●
3 **CONTINUING ESSENTIAL SKILLS AND STRATEGIES**		
I Inflected Nouns with Spelling Changes (y to i, add -es)		●
R¹, T* Context Clues		●
R³ Classify and Categorize		●
⊡ Colorful and Descriptive Language		●

Alternative Strategies

Providing for Individual Differences
pp. T481–T487
● Reteach
● Reinforce
● Extend
● Maintain

KEY TO SYMBOLS
I — Introduced; ⊡ – Introduced and taught at an earlier level
R — Reviewed; numeral indicates frequency
T* — Tested in this unit and in end-of-book test; T – Tested in end-of-book test

Summary

While cleaning the garage, Daisy finds a toy canoe. Her father explains that it was given to him by Grandpa as a remembrance of a fishing trip during which they had a great time but caught no fish. Daisy's father invites Daisy to go fishing. When Daisy catches a fish, she insists on letting it go so that her fishing trip can be exactly the same as the one her father and her grandpa went on. The next day, Daisy's father presents her with a remembrance of their day together. He gives her a toy fish.

Universal Theme

A present can help us remember a special day.

Lesson Vocabulary

Key Words canoe, smaller, tied

Skill Word string

All words appear in the Word Helper.

Additional Materials

INSTRUCTION *Instructional Charts: 51–53
          Word Cards
          *Cooperative Learning Guidelines

LEP *Language Development Handbook,
     Grade 1*: pp. 1–52, 130

PRACTICE *Study Book*: pp. 99–103

RETEACHING *Another Look*: pp. 93–98

Integrating the Language Arts

WRITING *Think, Read, and Write*: pp. 34–35
        HBJ Writer's File: Levels 1–2
        *Holistic Writing Evaluation Checklist
         (Self, Peer, Teacher)

LANGUAGE/SPELLING *Language Arts Handbook, Grade 1*

READ ALOUD, READ ALONG, READ ALONE HBJ Young Readers' Library, Grade 1, see p. T407
For additional books, see p. T410.

*Appears in the *Teacher's ResourceBank*™*

1 Preparing for Reading

DEVELOPING SKILLS

Decoding

R¹   Identify initial correspondence /str/str
R²ₜ T   Identify initial correspondence /st/st

LEP For Limited English Proficient students, see the *Language Development Handbook,* Grade 1.

 PURPOSE Today you will read words that begin with the sounds the letters *st* and *str* stand for, as in *stop* and *string.* Knowing these sounds and letters will help you read unfamiliar words.

TEACH **Listen to this rhyme about some things that go together. When you know the rhyming word, join in with me.** Read the following to the students. Answers are in parentheses.

Queen and king,
Ball of ___. (*string*)
Sing and song,
Weak and ___. (*strong*)
Foot and hand,
Sit and ___. (*stand*)
Jump and hop,
Go and ___. (*stop*)

Watch as I write the words you said:

string   stand
strong   stop

Read the first column of words with me: *string, strong.* What three letters stand for the sounds you hear at the beginning of *string* and *strong*? (*str*) Have volunteers come to the chalkboard and draw a line under the letters *str.* **Now read the second column of words aloud with me: *stand, stop.* What two letters stand for the sound you hear at the beginning of *stand* and *stop*?** (*st*) Let volunteers come to the chalkboard and draw a line under the letters *st.* Encourage students to think of other words that begin with these same sounds. Add their words to the chalkboard.

Listen to the beginning sounds in the words I say. When you hear a word that begins like *strong*, show me you are strong by flexing your muscles. When you hear a word that begins like *stand*, stand up. Say the following: *string, stick, still, stripe, strawberry, stump, stem, straw, still, strange.*

Have students reread the words on the chalkboard.

PRACTICE AND APPLY Write the following on the chalkboard, omitting the underscores, or display Instructional Chart 51:

CHART 51

street   stump

1. <u>St</u>an walks up a <u>st</u>eep hill.
2. He has some <u>st</u>ring in his hand.
3. <u>St</u>an <u>st</u>ands very <u>st</u>ill.
4. "There is a <u>st</u>rong wind today," says <u>St</u>an.
5. Will <u>St</u>an fly his kite?

Have students read the sentences aloud with you. Call on volunteers to identify and underline the words that begin like *straw.* Let others draw a line under the words that begin like *stump.* Have students read each underlined word aloud as you point to it.

Call their attention to the word *string.* **We will read the word *string* in the next story.** Let volunteers reread the sentences to the group.

SUMMARIZE The letters *str* stand for the sounds we hear at the beginning of *string* and *strong.* The letters *st* stand for the sounds we hear at the beginning of *stand* and *stop.*

For additional practice, you may want to use the activity "Fish." See *Teacher's ResourceBank™, Teacher's Bonus Book,* "Classroom Ideas."

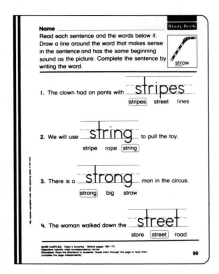

Name _____   Study Book

Read each sentence and the words below it.
Draw a line around the word that makes sense
in the sentence and has the same beginning
sound as the picture. Complete the sentence by
writing the word.

 straw

1. The clown had on pants with __stripes__.

   (stripes)   street   lines

2. We will use __string__ to pull the toy.

   stripe   rope   (string)

3. There is a __strong__ man in the circus.

   (strong)   big   straw

4. The woman walked down the __street__.

   store   (street)   road

SAND CASTLES, Daisy's Surprise. Before pages 166-175
Objectives: Identify initial correspondence /str/-str.
Directions: Read the directions to students. Guide them through the page or have them
complete the page independently.   99

S Bk 99 *Study Book* page 99 may be used for more practice. Read the directions to students. Then direct them through the page or have them complete it independently.

  For students who need additional instruction, see "Providing for Individual Differences," pages T481–T487.

Comprehension

R¹ Draw conclusions

PURPOSE Today we are going to use story clues and what we already know to figure out why people do things in a story.

TEACH In the last story, "The Giant Trees," the people decided to stop cutting down the giant sequoia trees. **Why did they decide to save these giant trees?** (They wanted to keep the forest beautiful; they wanted to save the trees because they were the biggest ones in the world.) **How do you know why they wanted to save the giant sequoia trees?** (It says so in the story.)

The story does give some reasons why the people saved the trees. Open your books again to page 162. Can you find any part of the story that says why the people wanted to save the trees? (Too many trees had been cut down. They took a long time to grow, people came to see them, they were the biggest trees in the world.) **Can you find any part of the story that tells why people think the sequoias are special?** (no) Nothing in this story tells us exactly why people think the sequoias are special. We have to use what we already know about people and what clues we have about sequoias to figure out why people think the giant trees are special enough to save.

Parts of the story on this page help us decide why people think the sequoias are special. This sentence gives us a clue: "The sequoias are the biggest trees in the world." To use this clue we have to think about what we already know. **Why do people go places each year to see things?** (to learn more, to see unusual things, to see things that are one of a kind) We know that sometimes people like to go see things that are beautiful or unusual. The clues in this story help us remember what we know about why people go places to see things. The sequoias are unusual because they are very old and because they are the biggest trees in the world. These clues help us understand that people like to go see special, one-of-a-kind things that are unusual. Trees like the sequoias are just that kind of thing to see. The clues in the story tell us that. What we know about why people go places to see things helps us use these clues about sequoias to figure out more about why people in a story do things like saving trees.

When we read "Daisy's Surprise," we will get a chance to figure out why Daisy does some things. We will have to read for the clues and think about what we already know, if we want to figure out Daisy's thoughts about her surprise.

PRACTICE AND APPLY Practice and application will occur both during and after reading the selection. See questions that accompany student pages and "Apply the Skill" in Step 2 of this lesson plan.

Vocabulary

I,T★ Identify lesson vocabulary

KEY WORDS canoe, smaller, tied
PROPER NOUN Daisy

PURPOSE Today you will learn new words that you will read in the next story in *SAND CASTLES*.

TEACH Write the following words and sentences on the chalkboard or display Instructional Chart 52.

CHART 52

Daisy

1. canoe   2. smaller   3. tied

1. Father was going out to catch fish.
   Daisy held the boat as he got in.
   She pushed the <u>canoe</u> out onto the river.
2. Father and the <u>canoe</u> looked <u>smaller</u> and <u>smaller</u> as they went away from her.
3. "I should have <u>tied</u> a rope to the canoe so I could pull it back."

Point to the name *Daisy* at the top of the chart as you say it. **You will read about a girl named Daisy.** Call on individual students to read the sentences aloud one at a time. As each sentence is read, have the student tell how he or she knew the underlined word.

Remind students to use the following strategies when they come to a word they do not recognize:

- listen carefully to the sentence;
- think about the sounds that the letters in the underlined word stand for;
- look for the word parts they know;
- say the word to themselves;
- look for meaning clues that might tell what the underlined word should be.

If the first volunteer recognizes *canoe* in sentence 1, ask how he or she knew the word.

If the underlined word is not recognized, prompt the students with phonics and context (syntactic and semantic) clues. Present the clues one at a time. For example, the underlined word in sentence 1 begins like *canary*; it names a kind of boat.

For sentences 2-3, use the following suggested clues one at a time.

2. This word begins with *small*; tells how the canoe looked to Daisy as it got farther and farther away. (*smaller*)
3. This word begins like *tired*; rhymes with *tried*; tells what Daisy wishes she had done with the rope to fasten it onto the canoe. (*tied*)

Have the sentences on the chalkboard or chart reread aloud.

Students will also read the words *catch, wind, held, end, sometime,* and *you've* in the selection. They should be able to decode these words independently by applying skills previously taught in the program.

PRACTICE AND APPLY To check the students' understanding of the new words, read the questions below to students. For each, have a volunteer come to the chalkboard or chart and point to the word that answers the question. Have the word read aloud.

1. Which word tells what someone did to get a knot? (*tied*)
2. Which word names a long, thin boat that is very light on the water? (*canoe*)
3. Which word tells that one thing is not as big as something else? (*smaller*)
4. Which word is a girl's name? (*Daisy*)

SUMMARIZE The underlined words in the story on the chalkboard or the chart are new words you will read in the next story in *SAND CASTLES.* Recognizing these words will help you read that story.

VOCABULARY CHECK If you wish to review the lesson vocabulary before students read the selection, have several students select word cards found at the end of *Another Look* and make up sentences that use the words. Any additional instructional time should focus on words that still seem difficult for the students. You may want to read aloud each sentence on the chalkboard or chart which contains one of these words and omit the underlined word. Call on students to pick the word which belongs in the sentence. Review phonics and context clues that help tell what the words are.

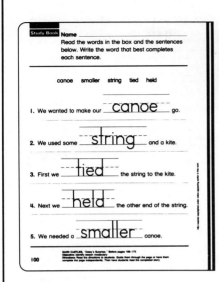

S Bk **Study Book** page 100 may be used for more
100 practice. Read the directions to students. Then direct
them through the page or have them complete it
independently.

For students who need additional instruction, see
"Providing for Individual Differences," pages
T481–T487.

2 Reading and Responding to the Selection

Notes to the Teacher

Text Structure This realistic story describes a series of
experiences shared by a father and daughter. It is told in
the third person in chronological order.

Teaching/Thinking Strategies General (Predictions)
Sometimes students make very reasonable predictions
about what will happen next in a story, but their
predictions turn out to be incorrect. Discuss with
students the importance of making predictions and point
out that even wrong predictions, if thoughtfully made,
may actually help us learn more.

(Cooperative learning: student-generated questions)
Instead of following the model under "Directing and
Modeling the Reading Process" you may wish to have
students generate questions that will help to reset
purposes. These questions should help to show you that
students have a clear understanding of what they have
read and are able to make predictions about what will
follow.

After students have read the section for which they have
asked predicting questions, have them continue to ask
questions about whether or not their predictions were
correct—continue this procedure for the rest of the
lesson.

GUIDING THE READING/
THINKING PROCESS

Building on Prior Knowledge

Begin a discussion of souvenirs that bring back special memories by sharing one of your own personal experiences. Explain why the object reminds you of happy times. **Have you ever brought back something special from a trip? Has anyone brought something back to you?** You might wish to list students' responses on the chalkboard, listing their names, the objects and the experience. A good follow-up to the story would be a souvenir table to display with creative writing next to each object.

Setting Purposes/Predicting

Turn to the Contents pages and locate the title of the story, "Daisy's Surprise." On what page does this story begin? (page 166) **Turn to page 166 in your books. Let's read aloud the headnote and title. What surprise do you think Daisy's father will give her?** (Accept reasonable responses. He might give her a toy; he might give her a pet.) Record students' predictions on the chalkboard or on chart paper. You may want to refer to the predictions after the story has been read. Direct students to their books. *inferential: predict outcomes*

OPTIONS If you are going to guide the reading of the selection, follow the suggestions and questions under *Directing and Modeling the Reading Process*. If students are going to read independently, follow the suggestions under *Reading Independently*.

Reading Independently

Remind students who are reading the story independently that stories usually have characters who have problems to solve or decisions to make. Suggest that, as they read, they pause to remind themselves of the problem and to think about how it might be solved. Remind them that a discussion will follow their reading.

Daisy finds something that her grandpa gave her father long ago. What surprise will Daisy's father give to her? Why?

Daisy's Surprise

by Dolly Cebulash

As Daisy was helping her father clean, she found a tiny canoe.
"Look at this canoe, Dad," she said.
"It looks just like your big canoe."

Daisy's father laughed.
"So it does," he said, "but this canoe is much smaller.
Your grandpa gave me this canoe when I was a little boy."

"Why did Grandpa give you this toy canoe?" asked Daisy.

"Your grandpa took me fishing in his canoe many years ago," said her father.
"We didn't catch any fish that day. But we had a good time.
The very next day, he made me this smaller canoe out of wood.
He said that when I looked at the canoe, it would make me think of that day."

"Does it make you think of that day, Dad?" asked Daisy.

166   167

Directing and Modeling the Reading Process

Set Purposes/Predict (page 166)

What do you think Daisy finds? (Accept reasonable responses. She finds a canoe; she finds toys.) *inferential: predict outcomes*

Read page 166 to see what Daisy finds.

Confirm Predictions/Check Up (page 166)

1. **What did Daisy find?** (She found a tiny canoe.) *inferential: confirm predictions*
2. **How did Daisy find the canoe?** (She was helping her father clean the garage.) *literal: details*
3. **When did Grandpa give Father the tiny canoe?** (He gave it to him when he was a little boy.) *literal: details*

Set Purposes/Predict (page 167)

Why do you think Grandpa gave Daisy's father the tiny canoe? (Accept reasonable responses. He gave it to him for his birthday; he gave it to him because he was good.) *inferential: predict outcomes*

Read page 167 to find out why Grandpa gave Daisy's father the tiny canoe.

Confirm Predictions/Check Up (page 167)

1. **Read the part that tells why Grandpa gave Father the canoe.** ("'He said that when I looked at the canoe, it would make me think of that day.'") *inferential: confirm predictions*
2. **Why was that day so special?** (They had a good time, even though they didn't catch any fish.) *inferential: draw conclusions*

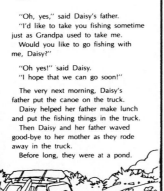

"Oh, yes," said Daisy's father.
"I'd like to take you fishing sometime just as Grandpa used to take me. Would you like to go fishing with me, Daisy?"

"Oh yes!" said Daisy.
"I hope that we can go soon!"

The very next morning, Daisy's father put the canoe on the truck.
Daisy helped her father make lunch and put the fishing things in the truck.
Then Daisy and her father waved good-bye to her mother as they rode away in the truck.
Before long, they were at a pond.

Daisy got out of the truck and looked at the pond.
She looked at the tall trees near the pond.
She heard the <u>wind</u> in the trees.
"What a pretty place," said Daisy.

"Yes, it's very nice here," said Daisy's father as he took the fishing things out of the truck.

169

Set Purposes/Predict (pages 168-169)

What do you think Daisy and her father will do next? (Accept reasonable responses. They will go fishing.) *inferential: predict outcomes*

Read pages 168 and 169 to find out what Daisy and her father will do next.

Confirm Predictions/Check Up (pages 168-169)

page 168

1. **What did Daisy and her father do next?** (They went fishing.) *inferential: confirm predictions*
2. **Read what Daisy's father asks Daisy.** ("'Would you like to go fishing with me, Daisy?'") *literal: details*
3. **When does the first day of the story end?** (After Daisy says, "I hope that we can go soon.") *inferential: sequence*
4. **How do you know that they will be gone a long time?** (They left in the morning and packed a lunch.) *inferential: draw conclusions*

Confirm Predictions/Check Up

page 169

1. **Where did they go to fish?** (They went to a pond.) *literal: details*
2. **How can you tell Daisy probably had not seen the pond before?** (She said it was a pretty place. It was the first time she had gone fishing with her father.) *inferential: draw conclusions*

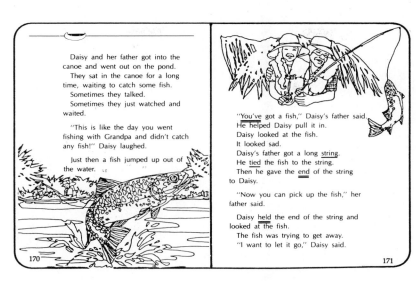

Daisy and her father got into the canoe and went out on the pond.

They sat in the canoe for a long time, waiting to catch some fish.

Sometimes they talked.

Sometimes they just watched and waited.

"This is like the day you went fishing with Grandpa and didn't catch any fish!" Daisy laughed.

Just then a fish jumped up out of the water.

170

"You've got a fish," Daisy's father said. He helped Daisy pull it in. Daisy looked at the fish. It looked sad. Daisy's father got a long string. He tied the fish to the string. Then he gave the end of the string to Daisy.

"Now you can pick up the fish," her father said.

Daisy held the end of the string and looked at the fish. The fish was trying to get away. "I want to let it go," Daisy said.

171

Set Purposes/Predict (page 170)

Will they catch a fish right away? Why? (Accept reasonable responses. Yes, because Daisy's father knew about the pond; no, because it will be the same as the fishing trip Daisy's father had with his father.) *inferential: predict outcomes*

Read page 170 to find out if they catch a fish right away.

Confirm Predictions/Check Up (page 170)

1. **Did they catch a fish right away?** (No. They waited a long time.) *inferential: confirm predictions*
2. **What did Daisy and her father do in the canoe besides fish?** (They talked; they watched and waited.) *literal: details*
3. **Why are they wearing life jackets?** (They want to be safe if the canoe tips over. The pond is deep. Perhaps one of them can't swim.) *critical: make judgments*
4. **Why was Daisy laughing?** (She thought they were not going to catch any fish just like the day her father and grandpa went fishing.) *inferential: draw conclusions*

Set Purposes/Predict (page 171)

How do you think Daisy will feel about catching a fish? (Accept reasonable responses. She will be happy; she will feel sorry for the fish.) *inferential: predict outcomes*

Read page 171 to find out how Daisy feels.

Confirm Predictions/Check Up (page 171)

1. **How did Daisy feel about catching the fish?** (She felt sorry for the fish and she wanted to let it go.) *inferential: confirm predictions*
2. **What did the fish do?** (The fish looked sad. The fish was trying to get away.) *literal: details*
3. **Was Daisy's father a good fisherman? How do you know?** (Yes, he helped Daisy pull the fish in. He tied the fish to a string.) *inferential: draw conclusions*

"I thought you wanted to catch a fish," said Daisy's father.

"I did," said Daisy, "but I wanted this day to be like the day you had with Grandpa."

"I see," her father said as he helped her take the fish off the string.
They dropped the fish back into the water and watched it swim away.

Soon it was time to go home.
Daisy and her father laughed about the fish as they rode home.
Daisy went right to sleep that night.
It had been a nice day!

172

The next day, when Daisy's father came home from work, he had a surprise for her.
It was tied with string.
"Open it," he said.

Before Daisy opened it, she said, "I think I know what it is.
It's a small canoe."

Her father just laughed.
When Daisy opened the surprise, she laughed, too.

Set Purposes/Predict (page 172)

What question might you ask about the next part of the story? (Accept reasonable responses. Why does Daisy want to let the fish go? Will her father allow her to let the fish go?) *inferential: predict outcomes*

Read page 172 to find out if your question is answered.

Confirm Predictions/Check Up (page 172)

1. **Did you find the answer to your question?** (Accept reasonable responses.) *inferential: confirm predictions*
2. **Why did Daisy want to let the fish go?** (She wanted the day to be like the day her father had with Grandpa. Accept reasonable responses based upon question and text.) *critical: make judgments*
3. **How do you know that her father understands how Daisy feels?** (He says, "I see," and helps her take the fish off the string.) *inferential: draw conclusions*
4. **Read the part that tells what a nice day it was for both Daisy and her father.** ("Daisy and her father laughed about the fish as they rode home." The last sentence on the page states, "It had been a nice day!") *inferential: draw conclusions*

Set Purposes/Predict (page 173)

Look at the picture on page 173. What is happening in the picture? (Accept reasonable responses. Daisy has a gift from her father. She is happy.) *inferential: predict outcomes*

Read page 173 to find out what is happening.

Confirm Predictions/Check Up (page 173)

1. **What happened next in the story?** (Daisy's father brought her a surprise.) *inferential: confirm predictions*
2. **Why does Daisy think it is a canoe?** (Grandpa had given her father a canoe after they went fishing together.) *inferential: cause and effect*

"Oh, Dad," said Daisy, "it's not a canoe.

It's a toy fish, just like the fish I got at the pond."

"When you look at this fish, I hope you will think of our day," said her father.

"Thank you, Dad!" Daisy said as she hugged her father.

"This will always make me think of our day at the pond!"

174

Discuss the Selection

1. What surprise did Daisy's father give her? Why?

2. Why did Daisy think the surprise from her father was a small canoe?

3. What happened when Daisy and her father went fishing?

4. How did you feel when Daisy opened the surprise?

5. When did you first begin to know that Daisy's surprise was not a canoe?

6. Why were the toy fish and the canoe both special?

175

Set Purposes/Predict (page 174)

What do you think the surprise will be? Why? (It will be a toy canoe. It will be something different.) *inferential: predict outcomes*

Read page 174 to find out what Daisy's surprise is.

Confirm Predictions/Check Up (page 174)

1. **What did Father give Daisy?** (He gave her a toy fish.) *inferential: confirm predictions*
2. **Why did Daisy laugh when she opened the package?** (She was surprised that it was not a canoe.) *inferential: cause and effect*
3. **What does her father hope she will do with the fish?** (He hopes she will think of their day together when she looks at the fish.) *literal: main idea*

EVALUATING COMPREHENSION/ RESPONDING TO THE SELECTION

Discuss the Selection

Remind students to think carefully before answering the questions. Encourage them to refer to pages of the selection if they wish.

1. **What surprise did Daisy's father give her? Why?** (He gave her a toy fish because he wanted to give her something to remind her of the fishing trip.) *literal: details (purpose)*
2. **Why did Daisy think the surprise from her father was a small canoe?** (Daisy thought her father gave her a canoe just like the one his father gave to him.) *inferential: draw conclusions (point of story)*
3. **What happened when Daisy and her father went fishing?** (They didn't catch anything for a long time. Then Daisy caught a fish and threw it back because she wanted the day to be like the day her father spent with his father.) *literal: sequence (summary)*
4. **How did you feel when Daisy opened the surprise?** (Answers will vary. I was surprised, too. I was happy for Daisy.) *critical: make judgments (reaction)*

Daisy's Surprise, pages 166–175   **T473**

5. **When did you first begin to know that Daisy's surprise was not a canoe.** (Accept reasonable responses. When her father laughed. When Daisy laughed.) *inferential: draw conclusions (metacognitive)*
6. **Why were the toy fish and the canoe both special?** (They helped Daisy and her father remember special times.) *inferential: draw conclusions (theme)*

These additional questions may be used to extend the students' critical and creative responses to the selection.

- **Why wasn't anyone else asked to go fishing with Daisy and her father?** (They wanted the day to be like the day Daisy's father had had with Daisy's Grandpa.) *critical: draw conclusions*
- **How do you know that Daisy's family lives near water?** (They own a canoe. They could get there by truck.) *critical: draw conclusions*
- **Do you think Daisy should have thrown the fish back? Why?** (Accept reasonable responses. Yes, she felt sad for the fish; she wanted the day to be the same. No, the day could not be the same.) *critical: make judgments*
- **Why was the toy fish a better choice than a canoe for Daisy?** (She would remember the day better because she caught a fish and let it go.) *critical: draw conclusions*

Review students' ideas generated prior to reading the selection before asking the following question:

- **Now that you've read the story, do you think the reason people collect souvenirs is a good one?** (Accept reasonable responses.) *critical: make judgments*

Summarize the Selection

S Bk 101   Now you are going to summarize the story. *Study Book* **page 101 will help you remember what happened in the story.** Remind students to refer to the selection when necessary. Provide assistance as needed.

Apply the Skill

R¹   Draw conclusions

PRACTICE AND APPLY   Why did Daisy let the fish go in the story "Daisy's Surprise"? (She felt sorry for the fish, she wanted the day to be like the day her dad had when he didn't catch a fish.) **How do you know that is the reason?** (The clues in the story let you know; the story said so.) **Let's find the clues in the story that help us figure out why Daisy let the fish go. Open your books to the story and tell us a page number that would have a clue.** (pages 171 and 172 relate the incident of throwing the fish back.) Write the clues that the students find on the chalkboard.

The fish was trying to get away.
"I want to let it go," Daisy said.

"I did," said Daisy, "but I wanted this day to be like the day you had with Grandpa."

They dropped the fish back into the water and watched it swim away.

Have you ever seen anyone catch a fish, then throw it back into the water? From what you already know, why would someone throw a fish back? (They were fishing just for fun, not for food; they didn't want to kill the fish; the fish was too little to keep.) **Do any of the clues we found about Daisy's fish fit best with what we already know about throwing fish back?** ("The fish tried to get away" fits with not hurting the fish; "wanting this day to be like the one you had with Grandpa" fits with fishing just to have fun.)

Why does Daisy want the day fishing with her father to be just like the day her father had with Grandpa? (Answers will vary. Relate to wanting a special day with her father that she can always remember, to her love for her father.) **Let's find the clues in the story that show Daisy's reasons for saying this when she throws the fish back. When you find a page with a clue, tell us.** (page 167 "'Does it make you think of that day, Dad?' asked Daisy"; page 168 "'Oh yes!' said Daisy. 'I hope that we can go soon'"; page 170 "'This is like the day you went fishing with Grandpa and didn't catch any fish!' Daisy laughed"; page 174 "'Thank you, Dad!' Daisy said as she hugged her father. 'This will always make me think of our day at the pond!'")

What do you already know that helps this clue make you think that Daisy wanted her day with her father to be just like his day with Grandpa? (Answers will vary, but should generally focus upon wanting to have special times with the people you love.)

SUMMARIZE   People in a story do many things and don't tell us exactly why. **When we read we should try to figure out why they do these things. We should try to figure out how they are thinking. How do we figure this out?** (We use the clues in the story, what they say and do, and what we already know about why people do things.) **If we use the clues in the story and what we already know about why people do things, we can figure out why people in a story do what they do.**

Study Book page 102 may be used for more practice. Read the directions to students. Then direct them through the page or have them complete it independently.

MOVING BEYOND THE LITERATURE

OPTIONS   Select one or more of the following activities according to the needs and interests of students. See also *Think, Read, and Write,* pages 34–35, as an alternative to the "Think and Write" activity.

Think Write

This activity correlates reading and writing. You may elect to use the writing as a homework or extra-credit assignment. You may also wish to have students use the *HBJ Writer's File* for the first five steps of the writing process. Remind students to keep in mind that before they begin to write they should have a clear purpose for writing. (Why are they writing and what do they hope to accomplish through their writing?) They should also keep their audience in mind. (For whom are they writing?) The following suggested steps are designed to help students better understand the writing process:

PREWRITE   Have students work with a partner to role-play Daisy getting the toy fish from her father. It may be helpful for students to reread pages 172–174. Have one student be Daisy and the other student be her father. Then have them switch roles. Tell students to think of what Daisy would write if she sent her father a thank-you note.

DRAFT   Ask students to think about a special gift they have received. Have them send a thank-you note to the person who gave them the gift. If they have not received a special gift, ask them to imagine they received something they have wanted for a long time. In their note they are to tell why the gift was special. Simplify the thank-you note to include only the heading:

   Dear ___.

CONFER/RESPOND   *Student/Student Conference (peer, small group, or class)*   Encourage students to share their work and remind them to respect the integrity of each other's writing. As students confer, encourage the writer to first tell about his or her thank-you note and then read it aloud. Stress the need for good communication among students as a means of fostering self-correction. The writer as well as the listeners should ask questions about the note. During the conference time, students might focus on one or two of the following points:

- Praise each other's writing by stating what they like about the piece;
- Ask questions to clarify any points or parts of the note that seem unclear, and offer suggestions to help improve the note;
- Discuss whether or not the note has a beginning, middle, and end;
- Discuss whether or not the note meets the assignment.

REVISE   Have students proofread their thank-you note to make sure their heading has capitals and they've put a comma after the person's name.

EDIT AND PROOFREAD   Select the appropriate editing and proofreading checklists in the *Teacher's ResourceBank™ Teacher's Bonus Book*, and have students edit their work based on the checklists.

EVALUATE   Through observing and evaluating students' writing in a variety of situations and at different stages of the writing process, you can gather data that will help you follow students' writing development. In addition to taking notes about each student's writing development and saving students' work during the course of the year, you may wish to use the Holistic Evaluation Forms found in the *Teacher's ResourceBank™, Teacher's Bonus Book*. Select the form that corresponds to the rater (self, peer[s], or teacher).

PUBLISH   Have students read their thank-you notes to a partner. If they are thanking someone for a real gift they have received, have them give the thank-you note to that person.

Expand Vocabulary and Concepts

Synonyms, Antonyms, and Comparatives

Have the students turn to page 166 in their books. Ask a student to read the first sentence in the story. ("As Daisy was helping her father clean, she found a tiny canoe.) Ask students to think of other words that mean the same as *tiny*. (*small, little*) Then ask students to locate the word that means the opposite of *tiny* on the page. (*big*) Ask students to think of more words that mean the same as *big*. (*huge, large, great*) Discuss how the author of the story compares the two canoes by using words that are opposite. Guide students in thinking of more synonyms, antonyms, and comparative words as you list them on the chalkboard.

Develop Fluency in Oral Reading

Establish Mood

The author creates a quiet mood in the scene at the pond before the fish is caught. Have students turn to page 169 in their books. **The feeling here is quiet. If I read this aloud in an excited voice, the mood is wrong.**

Listen as I read the part of the story that takes place at the pond in an excited voice. "Daisy got out of the truck and looked at the pond. She looked at the tall trees around the pond. She heard the wind in the trees." Now listen as I reread the same sentence in a quiet voice to show the quiet mood. Reread the same sentence to students, but this time use an appropriate tone of voice. Discuss with the students the sound of wind in the trees away from city and street noises. **This is the way the author makes the reader realize the quiet setting at the pond.** Have the students turn to page 170 in their books. **Here is another quiet part of the story. "They sat in the canoe a long time, waiting to catch some fish. Sometimes they talked. Sometimes they just watched and waited."** Have students take turns reading this paragraph in an appropriate tone of voice.

Reading Across the Curriculum

You may wish to choose from the "Ongoing Activities," found at the beginning of this unit, or the "Cross-Curricular Activities," found at the end of Step 3 of this lesson plan.

3 Continuing Essential Skills and Strategies

Decoding

I Identify inflected nouns with spelling changes (y to i, add -es)

PURPOSE Today you will read words that mean more than one, such as *cherries, stories,* and *daisies.* Knowing about the spelling changes will help you when you read unfamiliar words.

TEACH Close your eyes as you listen to this verse. See if you can imagine what you hear. Read the following to the students:

Butterflies flutter
Over the hill.
Daisies and clover
Bloom by the hill.
Canaries sing songs
On your windowsill.
The wind tells you stories
When you sit very still.

Watch as I write some of the words from the rhyme on the chalkboard. Write the following: *butterflies, daisies, canaries, stories.* **Read these words with me. All of these words mean more than one. They all have the** *-es* **ending.** Have volunteers come to the chalkboard and draw a line under the *-es* ending in each word. **Now, watch as I write the word that means one of each of these words.** Write the words *butterfly, daisy, canary,* and *story* next to each plural form. Have students read these words aloud with you. **All of these words mean one of something.**

Look at the words *butterfly* **and** *butterflies.* **What is different about these two words?** (*butterfly* tells that there is one butterfly; *butterflies* tells that there is more than one butterfly; they are spelled differently) **Look at the word** *butterfly.* **What letter is at the end of this word?** (*y*) **When a word ends with a consonant and the letter** *y,* **we change the letter** *y* **to** *i* **before we write the** *-es* **ending.** Call on volunteers to use each word in a sentence.

Look at the words *daisy* **and** *daisies.* **What has happened to the word** *daisy* **to make it mean more than one?** (The letter *y* is changed to *i* and *-es* is added.) **How do we know to change the** *y* **to** *i* **before writing the** *-es* **ending?** (The word *daisy* ends with a consonant and the letter *y.*) Let volunteers use each word in a sentence.

Discuss the remaining pairs of words in the same way. Let students take turns making sentences with both forms of the word. Have students reread all the words on the chalkboard. Call on volunteers to tell the words that mean more than one.

PRACTICE AND APPLY Write the following on the chalkboard or display Instructional Chart 53. Answers are in parentheses.

CHART 53

1. Meg looks at the little <u>canary</u>.
2. She likes to hear all the _____ sing. (*canaries*)
3. Todd will pick the yellow <u>daisy</u>.
4. He puts it in a vase with the other _____. (*daisies*)
5. Rita sees a <u>butterfly</u> in the garden.
6. She knows many _____ will come in the spring. (*butterflies*)

Have students read each sentence pair aloud with you. Call students' attention to each underlined word. Help students write the plural form of the underlined word to complete each sentence pair. Have students reread the completed sentences aloud with you.

SUMMARIZE When a naming word ends with a consonant and the letter *y,* change the letter *y* to *i* before adding the *-es* ending.

For students who need additional instruction, see "Providing for Individual Differences," pages T481–T487.

Vocabulary

R¦ T★ Use context clues

PURPOSE You are going to learn how to use the clues in a story to help you figure out the meanings of words. This will help you understand what you read.

TEACH Sometimes when you are reading you will come to a word and you will not be sure of its meaning. There are a number of clues that you can use to help you figure out the meaning of a word.

Turn to page 166 in your book. The word *canoe* is one that you read in the story. Pretend that you did not know the meaning of *canoe* and let's see how you might have figured it out. There are many clues on the first few pages of the story to help you figure out what a canoe must be.

The first two lines of the story tell us that Daisy found a tiny canoe while she was cleaning. How does the picture on the page give us a clue about the word *canoe*? (There is a picture of Daisy holding a small boat. The picture shows us what she has found.)

We are told that there are also big canoes and that people go fishing in them. These clues give us a pretty good idea of what a canoe must be. Let's put these clues together. The toy was a model of a big canoe; we can see the toy in Daisy's hand; people go fishing in canoes. What could a canoe be? (a type of boat)

Remember to pay attention to all the clues in a story. They can help you to figure out the meaning of a word.

PRACTICE AND APPLY   I will tell you a story. In the story there will be a word that you will not know because it is not a real word. If you listen carefully, you will be able to figure out a meaning for that word that will make sense in the story. Read the following:

Ted worked hard polishing his brand new Mardle. He stood back and looked at it carefully. Each part on the Mardle gleamed.

Ted decided to take it for a spin. He climbed on, grasped the handlebars and started it up. The Mardle roared to life. Pulling on his helmet, Ted turned it around and headed down the driveway. He loved the feeling of the wind as he rode through the city streets.

While he was riding, Ted saw Bob, a friend of his. He pulled over to the curb and Bob climbed on the Mardle behind Ted. "I see you got a brand-new Mardle," said Bob.

Ted just grinned. The two of them rode off, the engine of the Mardle roaring loudly.

Who can tell me what a Mardle is? (a motorcycle) **How do you know that it's a motorcycle? What clues are there in the story?** (Ted polished it; it has handlebars; it's something you ride; it can carry two people—one behind the other; you wear a helmet when you ride it; it has a loud engine.) **There are a lot of clues in that story to help you understand what a Mardle is.**

SUMMARIZE   Would it be a good idea to stop reading every time you come to a word that you don't know? (no) **Why?** (You don't have to stop reading because the story may have clues that will help you figure out the meaning of a word you do not know.)

S Bk 103   *Study Book* page 103 may be used for more practice. Read the directions to students. Then direct them through the page or have them complete it independently.

For students who need additional instruction, see "Providing for Individual Differences," pages T481–T487.

Name _____

Read each sentence and the words below it.
Fill in the circle in front of the word that begins
with the given letter and best completes each
sentence.

1. This small s_____ will grow into a tree.
   ○ sign   ○ plant   ● seed

2. I think a bird's n_____ is in that tree.
   ● nest   ○ home   ○ new

3. Today we are going to the c_____ .
   ○ come   ○ park   ● circus

4. We'll see some f_____ clowns.
   ● funny   ○ giant   ○ faces

5. Many dinosaurs were g_____ animals.
   ● giant   ○ going   ○ tall

6. A dinosaur was bigger than a h _____ .
   ○ here   ● hippo   ○ cow

7. Pam likes to swim in the s_____ .
   ○ sun   ○ water   ● sea

8. She has fun jumping in the w_____ .
   ● waves   ○ sand   ○ wait

SAND CASTLES, "Daisy's Surprise," After pages 169–175
Objectives: Use context clues
Directions: Read the directions to students. Guide them through the page or have them complete the page independently.

103

R⁵   Classify and categorize

PURPOSE   Today you are going to organize things that go together into categories or groups. You are going to see how some things are the same and some things are different. Recognizing this will help you understand what you are reading.

TEACH   Families enjoy doing things together. You are going to put words into a group that remind you of something families do together. Daisy and her father went fishing. Write *Fishing Words* on the chalkboard as a heading. I'm going to say three words. I want you to tell me the words that remind you of fishing: *canoe, hook, plane.* (canoe, hook) Write those words under the heading. **What are some other fishing words?** (string, pond, catch) Write the words that students suggest under the heading. **Would *fish* go on the list?** (yes) Write *fish* on the list. **Would *bulldozer* go on the list?** (no) Look at the new category you just made. Read all of the words under the category. **How do all of these words go together?** (They are all fishing words.)

I'm thinking of another category. It is something that families do together. Listen to these words: *blanket, food, basket.* Can you tell me what category I am thinking of? (Accept responses in relation to going on a picnic.) Write the heading *Picnic Words* on the chalkboard. Write the words *blanket, food,* and *basket* under the heading. **Can *cup* go on this list?** (yes) Write *cup* under the heading. **Why does *cup* go on the list?** (because you need cups on a picnic) **Does *picnic table* go on the list?** (yes) Write *picnic table* under the heading. **Does *parade* go on this list?** (no) **Why not?** (because you don't need a parade on a picnic) **Look at the list.** Read the words to students. **These words all go together. They are all words that make you think of a picnic.**

I'm thinking of something else that families do together. I'm going to say three words. I want you to tell me which words go together: *pool, scissors, swimsuit.* (Pool and swimsuit go together.) **What is the heading of this category?** (swimming words) Write *Swimming Words* on the chalkboard. Write the words *pool* and *swimsuit* under the heading. **Can you think of some other words that make you think of swimming?** (suntan lotion, towel, diving board) Write the words students suggest under the heading. Read the list to students. **All of these words go together. What words tell how they are all alike?** (*Swimming Words*)

All of these categories are things families can do together. In each of these categories are words that remind us of things that families do together.

PRACTICE AND APPLY Make one large and five smaller circles on a piece of paper. Make three copies for each student. Write the heading *Families Play Together* on the chalkboard. **I am going to draw a large circle on the chalkboard with smaller circles touching the edges of the larger circle.**

We are going to make some family flowers. Draw a circle on the chalkboard. **What is something that families do together?** (For example: they go on a picnic) Write the word *picnic* in the circle. **What are some of the words that remind you of a *picnic*?** (basket, blanket, food) **These are the family flower petals.** Draw five smaller circles (petals) around the outer edge of the larger circle. Write the words *basket, blanket,* and *food* in three of those circles. **Can you fill up the family flower with picnic words?** (picnic table, cup, paper plates) **You now have a family flower. Where is the heading?** (in the center) **All of the petals are words that go with that heading.**

Now you are going to make your own family flowers. Cut out the large circle. Write your heading in that circle. Then cut out the smaller circles or petals. Write words that go with your heading in these petals. Glue the petals onto the center of the flower. You may make three family flowers. If students have trouble coming up with categories, point out the categories that they made together.

SUMMARIZE Some things go together. You made categories with groups of words. **How did you know how to choose words for these categories?** (The words had to go with the other words.) **You chose a heading to go with each list of words. What does a heading tell?** (It tells how the things in the list are the same.)

 For students who need additional instruction, see "Providing for Individual Differences," pages T481–T487.

Literature

☐ **Identify colorful and descriptive language**

PURPOSE This activity will help you recognize words that create a picture in your mind, which will help you understand what you are reading.

TEACH Write the following sentences on the chalkboard:

1. Father made me a canoe.
   Father carved me a tiny canoe out of wood.
2. She looked at the trees.
   She looked at the green trees around the small pond.

Writers draw pictures with words. To help you see pictures, they use words that describe how things look, feel, sound, taste, or smell. They also use words to describe how people do things. Listen as I read these sentences. Decide which one helps to create a picture in your mind. Read the first set of sentences. **Which sentence gives you a better picture of the canoe?** (the second one) **Which words describe what the canoe looks like?** (tiny, carved out of wood) Point to *made* and *carved* in the sentences. **The word *carved* gives you a better idea of what Father did than the word *made*.** Repeat the same procedure for the second set of sentences. **Which words describe what the trees and the pond look like?** (*green, small*)

PRACTICE AND APPLY Divide students into groups of two. Give each group a picture postcard or a picture from a travel brochure. Have each student in the group write a sentence that uses colorful language to describe the scene or something in the picture. After students write their sentences, have them read them to their partners. Partners might suggest colorful language that may be added to the individual sentences. Then have students read their revised sentences to the group.

SUMMARIZE Remember, as you read, look for words that describe how people or things look, feel, taste, sound, or smell. These words will help to create a picture in your mind.

CROSS-CURRICULAR ACTIVITIES

Arts and Crafts: Designing Postcards

Materials: 4″ × 6″ pieces of tagboard, 1 per student; markers

Purpose: Students will design and send picture postcards to the special people in their lives as mementos of times spent with them.

Directions: Have each student recall a time he or she enjoyed being with a friend or family member. Have students discuss why they enjoyed those times.

Have each student create a memento of the time he or she spent with another person by drawing a picture of himself or herself and the other person as they were when they were together. For example, a student may draw himself or herself shopping with a grandparent or watching a baseball game on TV with his or her parents. Have students make the picture postcards by drawing the pictures on tagboard squares.

Then have each student draw a line on the back of the postcard to make two 4″ × 3″ sections. Tell each student to write a short message on the left side of the card. The message may be to thank the person pictured on the front of the card for spending time with the student or just a friendly greeting.

Homework: Have each student bring to school a postcard postage stamp and the full name and address of the person to whom he or she is sending the postcard.

Have students address the postcard on the right-hand side of the back of the card and mail the cards.

Language Arts: Photo Journalism

Materials: camera, film, photo album

Purpose: Students will record events during the school year by taking pictures and organizing the photographs into a class album.

Directions: Have students discuss the saying "A picture is worth a thousand words." **Why do people take pictures? Of what do they take pictures? Why do people like to have their pictures taken or dislike to have them taken?** Allow students to describe some of their favorite pictures. **Why are they special? What do your families do with the pictures?**

Have students suggest reasons for taking classroom pictures. **What special events occur during the year that could be remembered with pictures? What daily events could be photographed?** Have students also discuss elements of an interesting picture. (The photographer must be close enough to the people being photographed so they can be seen clearly. Objects and scenery are usually more interesting when people are also included.)

Have students take turns photographing classroom events. Each student may be assigned a "picture day" during the month. On his or her assigned day, tell the student to consider what he or she would like to photograph for the album. Take additional pictures as warranted. Once the pictures are developed, tell students to organize them chronologically into a photo album. Have students write captions for the pictures. Select pictures that may be used for future writing assignments.

Sharing Mementos

Purpose: Students will share with their classmates mementos from special events in their lives.

Directions: **In the story, Daisy's father gave her a small fish by which to remember their day at the pond. A reminder of the past is called a** *memento.* Have students brainstorm objects that might serve as mementos and their corresponding events. For example, a leaf could be a memento of a walk in the park, a postcard could be a memento of a trip, a T-shirt could be a memento of a historic place that was visited.

Homework: Have each student bring to school a memento of a special event in his or her life.

Have students share their mementos with the group. Allow students to describe the events, not simply the objects. Tell them to share with the group the reasons the events are special to them.

Decoding

Instruction Objective

Teaching the principle that when there are two vowels in a word, one of which is a final e, the first vowel has the long sound and the final e is silent (not sounded). Given a list of words following instruction on the final e vowel generalization, the student will be able to correctly mark the vowels and read words in context illustrating this generalization.

Readiness

We have discovered how vowel sounds can have the long sound, the short sound, or no sound, depending on where the vowels are located in a word. For example, we know the vowel o in the word *not* is short. Why is this sound found in many words? Good; one vowel in the middle of a word usually has the short sound. Today, we will learn another vowel combination to help you pronounce new words as you read.

Step-By-Step Explanation

Let's look at the two rows of words on the board:

not	note
bit	bite
pet	Pete
hat	hate

cut   cute
pin   pine

(Read the words in the first row and then those in the second row. Review the generalization illustrated in the first row by having students state the generalization, then ask students why the sound of the vowel changed in the second row.) Right; it has more than one vowel. (Review the new vowel generalization.) How many vowels are there in each word? Are they together? What is the last vowel? (Ask students to state the vowel generalization governing the words in the second row. Next ask students for additional words representing this vowel combination, and use each word in a complete sentence.)

Guided Practice

Write a new list of words representing this vowel generalization on the board.

plane   plan
bat   sad
paste   plate
bag   grade
same   wake
met   game

Engage in a rapid question-and-answer sequence regarding the new generalization (including others previously taught): "How many vowels are in the word? Where is the vowel located? Pronounce the word." After you are satisfied students can apply the vowel generalization to the new words, provide them with independent activities to ensure that they know the new generalization and can apply the new vowel combination in context.

Independent Practice

1. Write the following list of words on the board:

hope   sea   plate
plane   spoke   snake
rabbit   smile   cut
ripe   mat   soap

Ask students to copy the words on a sheet of paper and then mark the vowels long, short, or silent. Afterward, ask the students to pronounce each word, tell what it means, use it in a sentence, and discuss the vowel generalization.

2. Provide students with the following exercise to apply their vowel generalizations in context:

   Fill in the correct word in the blank in each sentence:

   plane   paste   pine   pale   pet   pay

   1. Tim loved the _____ ride.

   2. The _____ tree was sixty feet tall.

   3. Our dog Lassie is a great _____.

   4. Her face was _____ after the game.

   5. Please _____ for my popcorn.

   6. The _____ is on the top shelf in the garage.

Extension Activity

Play the game "Hangman." Using three-by-five-inch cards with words written on them illustrating the vowel generalizations, ask a different student to name each word. Each time a student mispronounces a word, that child adds another section to the body of his or her own "hangman." The student to first complete his or her "hangman" loses the game.

Structural Analysis:
Compound Words

Instructional Objective

After instruction, students will be able to combine two words from a list to form a new compound word and will be able to write sentences using compound words.

Readiness

Look at the sentence on the board and follow the words carefully as I read the sentence. "The boy walked into the bedroom to see his goldfish." In this sentence, there are three words that are unusual because each of them is made up of two words. Each part of these three words can be a complete word by itself, or be added to another complete word. Who can find the words? Yes—*into, bedroom,* and *goldfish* are each made up of two words put together to form one word. These words are called *compound words.* Today we will be working with these words and learn how they are formed.

Step-By-Step Explanation

A compound word is simply one word that has been made by combining two words into one new word. You use several of these words in your games when you go out to P.E. classes. One example would be the word *baseball.* That is a sport played with a bat, ball, gloves, and other equipment. But if you take that word apart, the two small words have their own meanings.

Base means *bottom,* and *ball* means *a round object.* When you put these two words together, they make *baseball,* which has its own meaning. Let's see how many compound words we can think of that are names of sports. *Football, basketball,* and *softball* are all compound words. Copy these three words from the board in a column. Then divide your paper into two more columns and write the two words separately. Here are pictures of different objects. When you know what they are, raise your hand and tell the class. Now write the words on your papers just as we did with the sports words. What is the daily news written in? Yes, the newspaper. Does the word follow our guide? Here are the pictures of an airplane, firefighter, hand-cuff, and keyhole. Can you think of any more words that are compound words? Write these words into your notebook.

Look at the word *compound.* Is that a compound word? Why not? That's right, *com* is not a word all by itself. It is a prefix. There are some words that will look like compound words, but when you use the guide, you will see that they are not words by themselves.

Independent Practice

Look at the worksheet on your desk. The first part of the sheet is a matching section. Look at a word in the first column and see if you can find a word in the second column that will go with it to make a compound word.

In the second section of the paper you are to circle the words that are compound words. Next write a sentence containing each compound word.

COMPOUND WORDS

I.   Match each word in the first column with a word in the second column to form a compound word. Put the letter of the word in the blank space in front of the second word. Select two of the compound words and draw a picture of them on another sheet of paper.

A. after   _____ father
B. barn   _____ room
C. bed   _____ side
D. air   _____ noon
E. birth   _____ line
F. him   _____ man
G. out   _____ yard
H. every   _____ plane
I. milk   _____ ball
J. in   _____ town
K. fire   _____ thing
L. some   _____ day
M. down   _____ self
N. grand   _____ to
O. foot   _____ place
P. under   _____ day

II.   Circle the words that are compound words.

babysit   pretest
sometime   ballpark
classroom   chalkboard
unlike   cookbook
shoelace   anything
without   together

Extension Activity

Ask the students to find compound words, and pictures of things that are compound words, in old magazines from home or the library. Ask them to cut them out, paste them on a sheet of construction paper, and write a sentence using the compound word to describe each picture.

Structural Analysis: Opposites/Antonyms

Instructional Objective

Given a list of words following instruction, the students will be able to write the opposite, or antonym, of the word and use it in a sentence.

Readiness

You already know what opposites are. Who can give me some examples of opposites? Let's have Jimmy and Joey stand up and face each other. Now Jimmy will go to the front corner of the room and Joey will go to the opposite corner in the back of the room. Can someone explain to the class what the boys did to get to the opposite corners of the classroom? Were they facing each other when they started? Before they started to walk, what did they have to do? Yes, they had to turn away from each other and then walk in opposite directions. Now they are at opposite corners of the room. (The boys can now return to their seats.)

How many things can we see in the room that are opposites? In your notebook, make a list of anything in the room that you think is the opposite of something else. Today we'll be looking very closely at words that are unlike or different, and you'll use what you know about opposites to identify antonyms in your reading.

Step-By-Step Approach

Words that are opposite in meaning are called *antonyms.* Let's look at the words on the board: *round, tall, square, hard, short, soft.* Let's make pairs of words that are different or opposite from each other. (Make a paired list on the board as the students give various answers.) Can you give me more pairs of words that are antonyms? (Review together how each pair of words is opposite as the students copy the list. Remind students it is important to know word opposites for three reasons: (1) Their vocabulary will grow; (2) their understanding of what they read will increase; (3) their writing skills will increase.)

Guided Practice

Let's look at the sentences on the board:

Baseball is a <u>funny</u> game.

The snow is very <u>heavy</u>.

Our car is <u>old</u>.

The story is <u>short</u>.

Joe gave me a <u>friendly</u> look.

Write these sentences in your notebook. For each underlined word, think of a word that is opposite in meaning and write it above the underlined word. Let's do the first one together. What's the opposite of *funny*? That's right, *sad.* Complete the sentences and we'll go over them together.

Independent Practice

With your partner, you will be given five cards, each with a different word printed on one side. Together, you must think of an antonym of the word, and then write a sentence on the reverse side using the antonym.

Extension Activities

Write a "backward" story in which words printed in red should be replaced by their antonyms. For example, "The flag is red, *black,* and blue. It has 50 *moons* and 13 *circles* in it. It flies *under* buildings." Have the students correct the paragraph. Ask them to try writing such a sentence or a story.

Provide students with sentences containing target vocabulary words. In parentheses use two synonyms and one antonym. Have the student underline the antonym. For example: The villa (estate, mansion, shack) overlooked the ocean.

Comprehension: Finding the Topic Sentence

Instructional Objective

Given a series of paragraphs following instruction, the students will be able to select and write the topic sentences appearing at the beginning of a paragraph.

Readiness

We have been learning about the key words in a sentence. (Provide written examples of key words in sentences on the board as a review.) What are the key words in these sentences? What did we say a key word is? Today you are going to use what you learned about key words in sentences to pick out key sentences in a paragraph. If you can recognize the key sentence in a paragraph, you will be better able to understand what you are reading.

Step-By-Step Explanation

Let's turn our attention to the paragraph on the board. (Choose a paragraph from narrative or expository text.) You already know that all the words in a sentence are not equally important. Likewise, all the words in a paragraph are not equally important. Now, do you think every sentence in a paragraph is equally important? Good; all sentences are not of equal importance. Usually, one sentence in every paragraph contains the whole or main or key idea of the paragraph. (Direct students' attention to the paragraph written on the board. Read the paragraph aloud and ask if someone can identify the one sentence that gives the main idea of the paragraph. Underline the topic sentence and circle the remaining sentences.) This sentence is called the *topic sentence* of the paragraph. It's very important for you to know what a topic sentence is and how to find it in a paragraph. The topic sentence is usually the most important sentence in a paragraph because it has in it the main idea of the paragraph. In each of your school textbooks and in the stories you read, there is a lot of material that you don't have to remember—but you must be able to understand the key or main idea of what you are reading. If you are skillful at finding the topic sentence, you will not have to spend too much time with the details. In many paragraphs, the main idea is so simple that you could understand the paragraph by finding and reading the one sentence that is the topic sentence. Now, looking at the paragraph on the board, what is the function of the sentences other than the topic sentence? That's correct; the other sentences in a paragraph have a direct connection with the topic sentence. They usually tell the *why* and *how* of the topic sentence. They give more information about the topic sentence. Most of the time the topic sentence is the first sentence in a paragraph. However, the topic sentence can be in the middle or at the end of the paragraph. Also, some paragraphs do not have a topic sentence, and you have to summarize the main idea yourself from the information provided. Today we will look at topic sentences at the beginning of a paragraph only.

Guided Practice

(Create a worksheet listing several paragraphs. Some should have their topic sentence appearing at the beginning; others should have no topic sentence whatsoever.) Let's look at the first paragraph on your worksheet together. Now I'd like you to read this paragraph to yourself and underline the topic sentence. Does this paragraph have a topic sentence? Where is it? Why is the first sentence the topic sentence? What do the other sentences tell? Very good!

Independent Practice

At this time I'd like you to read the rest of the paragraphs silently and underline the topic sentence in each one. Not all the paragraphs will have a topic sentence. When you finish the exercise, go back to the paragraphs that did not have a topic sentence and write down what you feel the key or main idea is, using the details provided to you. When we are all through with the activity, we will go over each paragraph together.

Extension Activities

Direct students to read selected paragraphs from their social studies or science textbooks and to be prepared to state the topic sentence and how the supporting sentences relate to it.

Read short paragraphs aloud, and ask students to either single out the topic sentence or give the main idea in their own words.

Provide students with a series of paragraphs. After reading each paragraph, illustrate the main idea and supporting details by designing a semantic web (place the main idea in the center, with details radiating out as threads).

Comprehension:
Hypothesizing

Instructional Objective

Following a discussion of hypotheses as a possible solution to a problem, students will know the importance of hypothesizing and be able to collect information and present an oral report on a hypothesis on the origin of the solar system.

Readiness and Discussion

Does anyone know the answers to the following questions:

- Why does a giraffe have a very long neck?

- Why is Mike taller than George?

- Why do some students love science and others do not?

Do we have only one specific answer to these questions, as we do for the question, "Who is older, John or our principal, Mrs. Wild?" You are correct—there are several possible answers or explanations. These possible explanations or guesses are called *hypotheses.* When you provide an explanation for something, you are *hypothesizing.* Hypotheses are possible answers or solutions to a question or problem. Sometimes we can look up the correct answer to a problem in an encyclopedia. For example, to answer the question, "How big is the planet Venus?" you can go directly to an encyclopedia. But many times a problem or question does not have a single correct answer. In such instances, you may have a hunch that may explain the problem and propose a hypothesis—a guess based on some information or experiment. Most of the time there is more than one hunch or hypothesis for a problem. Going back to our initial questions, is there more than one hypothesis to explain them? Not only do you need to know what a hypothesis is, and be able to think of several possible solutions to a problem, you should also be able to collect information on a hypothesis, and decide from the information whether you agree with a possible solution.

Guided and Independent Practice

Today, we are going to apply our knowledge of hypothesizing to a very important question, one that has been of interest to the human race for thousands of years. This important question—or problem for which we don't have one single verifiable answer—is the origin of the solar system. Do you know any of the hypotheses that have been given as possible explanations for how our solar system was formed? Many hypotheses have been given through the ages. The transparency on the screen lists several hypotheses to explain the origin of our solar system.

1. Count de Buffon of France—1749

   A great comet collided with the sun, throwing off streams of gas in all directions. After millions of years, the gases shrank into ball-shaped planets.

2. German scientist and philosopher, Kant—1755

   A huge cloud of rotating gas spun faster and faster, throwing off rings that shrank into planets and their moons. The cloud at the center shrank greatly, became fiery hot, and formed the sun.

3. Frenchman, Laplace—1796

   As a great cloud spun, it bulged from the rotation and threw off nine rings, which eventually formed planets. What was left of the original gas in the center became the sun.

4. American scientists, Chamberlin and Moulton—1895

   When the sun encountered another star, great quantities of gas were forced from the sun into space. The gas shrank into rocklike masses, later becoming planets and moons.

5. Englishmen, Jeans and Jeffrey—1917

The sun encountered another star, causing a great tidal bulge in the sun's surface. This bulge split off and broke up to form planets.

6. German astronomer, von Weizsacker—1944

When a great cloud of gas and dust began shrinking, it became hot enough to form the sun. The remaining gases around the sun formed whirlpool-like eddies that shrank to form planets.

Now get in your groups (cooperative groups assigned by the teacher), and I want each group to study one assigned hypothesis, locate sources of information in our library, read about it, and discuss it together. Later we will have each group give an oral report on their hypothesis.

Extension Activity

Ask each student to formulate his or her own hypothesis about the origin of the solar system and then write a report on it. In addition, students can draw a picture using their imagination about how the solar system was formed. Students can then present an oral explanation of their hypothesis to the class.

Comprehension: Determining the Author's Viewpoint

Instructional Objective

Given a series of paragraphs following instruction, students will be able to determine the author's viewpoint (to inform, entertain, or persuade).

Readiness

Most of us do things for a reason. Why do people exercise? What are some other reasons? Why do you watch television? Why do you clean your room at home? As you can see, we do things for different reasons, but we almost always have a reason behind our actions. Today we are going to see that writers almost always have a reason for writing what they do. Also, it is very important for readers to determine a writer's reason, or purpose in writing. Being able to do so will help you better understand what you are reading and will make reading more enjoyable.

Step-By-Step Explanation

When you read—whether it is the front page of a newspaper, the sports page, a story, a magazine, or a textbook—you do so with a purpose or reason. I'm sure you rarely read without a purpose in mind. Likewise, the author of anything you read wrote it with a specific purpose in mind. When an author's purpose is to give information, he or she is interested in providing facts that will inform or educate the reader. In other reading materials, the author is interested in entertaining the reader. In these cases, the author will share a tale of adventure or mystery or convey feelings and emotions to the reader. Still another purpose or viewpoint an author can express is trying to persuade you, the reader, to agree or disagree with a particular view. If a paragraph is written to persuade, there are certain key words that quickly point this out, like these: the *strongest*, the *best*, they *believe*. It is important to realize whether a writer is trying to win your support for an idea. Writing to persuade is most common during election campaigns and in advertisements. It is also important to realize that many times authors reveal more than one purpose or viewpoint in a single article. The old saying "Don't believe everything you read" means that you, the reader, need to recognize the author's purpose as you read. Let's listen to the following three paragraphs. After I read each paragraph, let's try to decide whether the author's purpose was to inform, to entertain, or to persuade.

> *The sailor drew up the anchor, hoisted the sail, and headed out into the open sea. The winds were with him and the sky was clear. He knew today the fish would be plentiful.*

> *On Sunday morning, December 7, 1941, the Japanese struck the United States naval base at Pearl Harbor in the Hawaiian Islands. The attack was a surprise to the Americans and destroyed a large portion of the U.S. Pacific Fleet.*

> *One of the best ways to keep your car looking new is to wax it three times a year. The wax will keep the car clean and shining.*

Guided Practice

At this time, let's read a few paragraphs silently and decide whether their purpose is to inform, to entertain, or to persuade. Write your answer after each paragraph. After you have finished, we will go over each paragraph together.

> *Are your hands rough and dry? When was the last time your husband held your hand? If you want to have soft, beautiful hands, start using Peterson's Pumice Puree on your skin today. It is the best cream available.*

Texas has a variety of climates. Precipitation is about 50 inches annually in the east and only about 10 inches in the west. In northern Texas, the average January temperature is 33 °F, while along the Gulf Coast it is 60 °F.

Hiking boots are the single most important piece of equipment a hiker must purchase. The best boots are all leather and have a thick rubber sole. Harry Hiker's boots use only the finest leather and the strongest rubber available. Most people agree they are worth the price.

Independent Practice

Read the following paragraphs and write the author's purpose (to inform, entertain, or persuade) at the end of each paragraph.

The first time I saw her walking toward the field, I couldn't believe my eyes. She was just over four feet tall with a very slender, almost fragile figure. Her long, curly hair was the color of wheat and her eyes an icy blue. Over the loudspeaker a voice said, "With a record of 12 and 1, pitching for the Winchester Mustang Little League, Elizabeth Drummond."

The Grand Canyon is one of the natural wonders of the world. It is a combination of gulches, ravines, canyons, and mountain peaks. It is four to eighteen miles wide, and the walls in some sections are more than 3,000 feet high.

It was a dark and moonless night, and the gusty winds rattled the old windows. We all heard the scratching noises coming from the room above us. Up the stairs we crept toward the room. My hand trembled as I turned the knob and flung the door open. In the middle of the room sat three fat rats munching on bits of cheese and bread.

When the boys left the dock in their sailboat, the sky was a beautiful blue with a few white, puffy clouds. Tim and Bill were about a mile out of the harbor when the wind started blowing very hard. The waves grew to huge swells, and the little boat was tossed around like a tiny buoy. Tim clung to the side of the boat while Bill clung to the wheel, trying to keep the boat upright. As suddenly as the wind began, it subsided and the sea again became calm. Tim and Bill smiled at each other with relief and continued their journey.

The United States spends billions of dollars a year on its space program. But the benefits reaped from such a program do not help the majority of our people. This money can be better spent in other ways, such as promoting economic growth in our cities. It could erase poverty in the United States. This money could be spent for medical research to find a cure for cancer, diabetes, muscular dystrophy, or any number of terrible diseases. Sending machines into space and men to the moon is exciting and impressive, but what lasting, helpful effect does it have on the people of the United States as a whole?

Extension Activity

Ask each student to read the daily newspaper, and cut out and bring to class one informative article, one entertaining article, and one persuasive article.

Comprehension: Cause-and-Effect Relationships

Instructional Objective

Given cause-and-effect statements following instruction, students will correctly identify cause-and-effect segments.

Readiness

After turning off and on the lights in the classroom, tell the children that one action (turning the switch off) caused another to happen (the lights went out). When reading, it is important to be able to identify cause-and-effect relationships in order to understand fully what one is reading. Many people have trouble deciding on the cause-and-effect parts of a statement. Today we will concentrate on some cause-and-effect statements that will help your ability to understand what you are reading. The following activities will help us with this skill.

Step-By-Step Explanation

Follow the sentence written on the board as I read it to you. "Because he left his book there, James is going back to his friend's house." Who can tell me what is going to happen in this sentence? James is going back to his friend's house. This is the effect, or the part of the sentence that tells what will happen. (Write on the board: What happens = effect.) Why did James go to his friend's house? He left his book. (Write on the board:

Why it happens = cause. Ask a student to come up to the board and underline the effect with the yellow chalk.)

Let's look at another sentence. "There was much damage and destruction because a tornado ripped through the town." What happened in this sentence? Yes, there was damage and destruction, and this is the effect. Why was there damage and destruction? Yes, because of the tornado. Underline the effect in this sentence. Remember the important rule: *What* equals effect, and *why* equals cause.

Guided Practice

Copy the first sentence from the chart into your notebook. "The book she wanted was not on the shelf, so she selected another one." Ask yourself what happened and why it happened, and then underline the cause with one line and the effect with two lines. What were the cause and the effect? Good; the cause was that the book was not on the shelf, and the effect was that she selected another book. Let's do the next sentence together. "The glass crashed to the floor as it slipped through her greasy fingers." Ask yourself the what and why questions, and underline the cause with one line and the effect with two lines. What were the cause and the effect? Put a star next to your sentence if you underlined twice "The glass crashed to the floor," because that is what happened. The rest of the sentence is the cause, or the *why.*

Try the last sentence on your own. "The baby cried and cried when he was hungry." What part of the sentence did you underline twice? Put a star by your sentence if you underlined "The baby cried and cried" twice.

Independent Practice

Here is a worksheet with five sentences. In each sentence, underline the cause once, and the effect twice.

1. Because the test was difficult, Chris had a hard time answering some questions.

2. The water stopped dripping when the plumber fixed the leaking faucet.

3. Pat won the race, so he grinned from ear to ear.

4. Richard wanted to make an A on his project, so he worked very hard on it.

5. She took courses every summer because she wanted to graduate early.

Extension Activities

Ask students to read the first five pages from their social studies book and find as many sentences as they can that contain a cause-and-effect statement.

Select or prepare several short paragraphs in which there is a final act. Ask the students to explain why the final act occurred.

Example: Jack slipped out of the house and ran to his favorite climbing tree. As he neared the top, a branch broke and he fell to the ground.

Question: What happened to make Jack fall? (A branch broke.)

Strategic Reading: Summarizing

Instructional Objective

Given sample paragraphs and a review of main idea, topic sentence, supporting detail, categorizing, and paraphrasing, the student will be able to write a summary of a paragraph using the reviewed skills.

Readiness

We have already learned main idea, topic sentence, and supporting detail. Who can explain what a main idea is? What is a topic sentence? What are supporting details? Who can tell me a category for the following items: shirt, slacks, socks, shoes, jacket? Clothing; very good! We already know how to categorize, don't we? You also know how to put an author's idea into your own words. Today we are going to use what you know about all these skills to learn something new called *summarizing.* We are going to learn how to summarize a paragraph. Later we will learn how to summarize entire sections of your textbooks. If you can summarize what an author has said, you will be better able to understand and remember what you are reading.

Step-By-Step Explanation

A summary is usually short and states only the most important ideas the author wants to express. A summary relays the same important *information* the author conveys, but uses different *words*. When we summarize, we not only use different words but might also want to put the ideas in a different order.

Before we can begin to summarize, we have to find the main idea, the topic sentence, and the supporting details. Look at the paragraph I have written on the board. Who would like to read this for us? Who can tell us what the main idea is? Let's write the main idea in our own words on the board. Who can read the topic sentence for us? Now let's write the topic sentence in our own words on the board. What are the supporting details in the paragraph? Let's look closely at those details. Some details are more important than others, aren't they? When summarizing, we want to eliminate the unnecessary details and focus on only the important ones. The next thing we want to do is look at the details and see if we can think of a word or phrase that explains or categorizes all the details. (For example, if the author uses supporting details such as pine, oak, maple, or cedar, the students might combine the details by referring to them as trees. If the listed trees were all deciduous, the students' phrase might be deciduous trees. Generate a list of words and phrases on the board. Discuss those that best describe the supporting details. Explain why some words or phrases provide more information than others.) Next we need to expand our word (or phrase) into a sentence or into a few sentences. (Record the students' sentences on the board.) Now we are ready to summarize. (Guide the students to combine their main idea, topic sentence, and summarized supporting details into a coherent paragraph. Record the final product on the board.) Let's read our summary.

Guided Practice

Let's try one more together. Read the first paragraph on your worksheet silently. What is the main idea? Write the main idea in your own words. (Check each student to see that each step is done correctly.) What is the topic sentence? Now write the topic sentence in your own words. What are the supporting details? Which ones are the most important? What word or phrase can you think of that best explains all the details? Write a sentence explaining your word or phrase. Now let's put all our sentences together. (Check each paragraph.)

Independent Practice

Next I'd like you to do the remaining paragraphs on your own. When you finish writing the main idea, topic sentence, and supporting details in your own words, put them all together in a paragraph. Do that for each paragraph; then I will check your work.

Extension Activities

Direct the students to read selected paragraphs from other content-area textbooks and then to summarize them orally.

Direct the students to read selected paragraphs from other content-area textbooks that have no stated main idea or topic sentence, and have them write a summary.

Vocabulary:
Polysemous
Words

Instructional Objective

Given vocabulary words in context, the student will be able to write multiple meanings of a given set of vocabulary words.

Readiness

We have been learning about new vocabulary words and context clues. Who can remind us what context clues are? You also know that when you read it is very important to think about everything you already know, that is, to use your background knowledge and experiences. Today we are going to learn about words that have more than one meaning. In order to do this, you will need to use your background experiences and what you know about context clues. If you know that words can have more than one meaning, you will be better able to understand what you are reading.

Step-By-Step Explanation

Let's begin by looking at the word *stick*, which I have written on the board. You already know this word, so you can use your background experiences to help you. Tell me all the meanings you can think of, and I'll write them on the board. (Some meanings include a piece of wood, pierce, adhere, stay with it.) Very good. Now let's look at the word *stick* and see how the meaning can change depending on the context. (Write *joy stick* on the board.) Who can tell me what a joy stick is? The context has changed the meaning here, hasn't it? Let's try some other phrases. (Depending on the students' background knowledge, choose appropriate phrases to write on the board, such as *stick to your guns, stick your neck out, stick-in-the-mud, stick out, stick shift, stick-to-itiveness, stick insect,* and *stick figure.*) Who can read these phrases for us? What do they mean? Here we can see how the context has affected the meaning of the word *stick.* Now let's see how we can apply what we know about words having more than one meaning to our reading. (Choose from four to six vocabulary words from a selection the students will be reading. The students must be able to determine the meanings of the chosen words through the use of context clues.) Take out a sheet of notebook paper and fold it into four columns. Label the first column *Words,* the second column *Meanings I Know,* the third column *Author's Meaning,* and the last column *Clue Words.* Copy the words I have on the board in the first column, leaving four or five blank lines between each word. Let's look at the paragraph I have written on the board. I have underlined your vocabulary words. They are the same words you have written on your paper. Next, tell me all the different meanings you know for our first word. Let's write those down in the second column, *Meanings I Know.* Who would like to read the first two sentences of the paragraph for us? What meaning did the author intend? Now we can write that in the third column, *Author's Meaning.* What were the clue words that helped you know the author's meaning? Good; let's write those in the last column, *Clue Words.* We can use what we already know along with context clues to help us understand the different meanings of words.

Guided Practice

Let's do the next word together. Read the next three sentences to yourself. Look at the underlined word. It's also the second word on your paper. Tell me the meanings you already know for this word. Good; let's write those in our second column. What meaning did the author intend? Yes, write the author's intended meaning in the third column. What were the clue words? (Discuss student responses.) Good; you need to write those words in the last column.

Independent Practice

At this time I'd like you to read the rest of the paragraph silently and continue filling out your sheet for the remaining vocabulary words. Do it just like we did when we worked together. When you finish, I'll check your work and we can talk about the different meanings you thought of.

Extension Activity

Direct the students to discuss the words that had surprising meanings and those words that matched the meanings they had recorded.*

---

*Adapted from Irwin, J.W. (1989). *Promoting Active Reading Comprehension Strategies: A Resource Book for Teachers.* Englewood Cliffs, NJ: Prentice Hall.

Functional Reading:
Using the Newspaper
to Promote Reading
Comprehension

Instructional Objective

Identifying significant details that support a main idea. Given a series of newspaper articles with the main idea contained in the headlines, students will be able to write and discuss main ideas and supporting details.

Readiness

I would like everyone to look at this mobile hanging from the light over my head. The phrase on the strip across the middle of the coat hanger says *Legendary Sports Heroes.* What are the words on the single strips hanging down from the coat hanger? Good; the names of Babe Ruth, Chris Evert, Wilt Chamberlain, Wilma Rudolph, Hank Aaron, and Muhammad Ali. Who are these people? Yes, they are sports figures who were stars in their sport. As seen on the mobile, the phrase on the strip across the middle is the central idea—*Legendary Sports Heroes*—and the names below it are supporting details. These supporting details, or in this case the names of sports heroes, tell about the central idea. When you read silently, it is helpful not only to identify the main idea but to be aware of and identify details supporting the main idea. By recognizing supporting details you will more easily understand what you are reading.

Step-By-Step Explanation

Using the newspaper is an excellent way to develop the skill of finding supporting details for a main idea. Let's look at the front page of today's paper. What is the first thing you notice when you look at the front page? That's right, the headlines. Why do newspapers have headlines? Good; they tell us what the article is about; in other words, they tell us the central or main idea of the article in a few words. For example, today's headline reads, "Avalanche Kills 40 Climbers in Soviet Central Asia." If the headline is the main idea of the article, what's an easy way of identifying the key or supporting details? What did we learn last week that a good reporter focuses on to give a clear and accurate account of an event? That's right; a reporter uses precise language and includes the five W's—*who, what, where, when, why*—and *how* if appropriate. The answers to these questions should provide us with the significant details. Let's read the article on the avalanche silently and we'll answer the W questions together. (Write the answers on the board under the headline.)

Guided Practice

Turning to the sports page, let's read the main headline and the article on the new football coach. Who can tell me the main idea? Fine; the local football team announced the hiring of a new coach. Now what are some of the significant, or key, details regarding this new coach? That's correct; now you are getting the hang of it.

Independent Practice

Let's work in pairs. I'd like each pair to read any two articles in our paper. Write out the main idea and supporting details of the articles on a piece of paper to share with the rest of the class.

Extension Activities

Have students, individually or in pairs, read a newspaper article about a person. Have students list the key words that best describe the person. Individually or in pairs, have students write their own newspaper article. Afterward, have each student or pair of students "teach" the article to the rest of the class, making sure the main idea and supporting details are identified.

Outline of an
Integrated Unit

Major Activity

Promoting and developing recreational reading through the celebration of Book Week.

Instructional Objective

Two- to three-month projects centered on the following major reading and language arts skills and abilities to be developed and reinforced:

- Extending students' reading interests
- Summarizing ideas
- Making comparisons
- Determining the author's purpose
- Letter writing
- Oral reporting
- Integrating the arts in language learning

Type of grouping: individual, whole, and cooperative.

Introduction

This project is planned around the celebration of Book Week, which occurs during the month of November each year. This whole class project is started in September, with culminating activities during Book Week. This highly motivating integrated reading/language arts unit can enliven the classroom environment and launch the year in an exciting fashion. The following activities are completed periodically during traditional reading, language arts, and art periods.

Activities

1. Discuss the whole idea of a class project occurring over two to three months. Emphasize both individual effort and teamwork as crucial to the success of the project. Next discuss the importance of recreational reading, including different types of books, authors, and the allocation of school and outside-of-school time for wide reading. Last, administer an interest inventory to all students to help in selecting library books for the classroom.

2. Initiate an intensive recreational reading program as soon as the school year begins, allowing students to read books of their choice. Also, as soon as possible, encourage students to choose their favorite book.

3. Form cooperative learning groups (heterogeneous in ability) to accomplish various purposes in the unit.

4. Have the students identify the author of their book and discuss what they would like to tell or ask the author if they had the opportunity to do so. Encourage the students as an entire class project to write a letter to their favorite authors. Replies from the authors (and many times the publishers as well) will be proudly displayed during Book Week. Give whole-class instruction on the basics of letter writing. In the cooperative groups, require each student to write a letter to the author of his or her favorite book. Cooperative groups work together on this activity, during which peer tutoring and cooperation between members of each team are emphasized. Encourage students to explain to the authors why they liked the books so much, and if they had a question about the story, encourage the students to ask the authors for an explanation. Have the students write preliminary drafts, rewrite, and polish their initial efforts in a team atmosphere. Send the letters by the end of September to ensure responses from the authors and publishers by Book Week.

5. Require a written book report on each student's favorite book (due at the end of October). The written reports should include a summary of the book, ideas and experiences in the book the student would like to share with others, descriptions of main characters, and events in the story that were the most interesting.

6. To aid in both the written book report and the oral report to be given at the Book Fair, provide direct instruction and much interesting and varied practice in the skills of summarizing, determining the author's purpose, and comparing. The primary vehicles to teach these skills will be the students' favorite books. Assignments associated with these skills will be completed in cooperative groups. Members of each group will work together on their books, comparing stories, characters, settings, plots, styles of writing, and summarizing the plots.

7. Have each student create a diorama depicting a particular scene from his or her favorite book. Using cardboard boxes as a shell, students may design their own scene using whatever materials are at their disposal.

8. As responses are received from the students' favorite authors, show off their personal letters on a bulletin board.

9. In preparation for Book Week, have the students practice two plays, giving special attention to public speaking and acting qualities. Examples of plays are *How a Book Is Made* and *How to Use the Library.* The Children's Book Council in New York is an excellent source for suggestions for plays, materials, posters, and suggestions for Book Fairs to celebrate Book Week.

10. As another instructional activity and bulletin board display before Book Week, ask students to prepare a book jacket and/or bookmark of their favorite book and to compose a telegram summarizing their book in twenty-five words or less.

11. In preparation for Book Week, have students (in cooperative teams) prepare and practice imaginative oral reports to present along with their dioramas.

12. Invite an author of children's books to speak to your class and the school assembly during Book Week. The appearance of such an author would be an attractive and beneficial

addition to the celebration. The author might also observe the work the students designed for Book Week.

Book Week

Activities of the celebration take place over at least three days. Reserve two days for the display of the dioramas and accompanying oral book reports: one day for other classes in the school to visit, and the second day for parents and central office administrators. Each student is positioned next to his or her diorama and delivers a short oral summary of the diorama and book. In addition, the classroom is decorated with bulletin boards made by the students, as well as various posters and art work celebrating Book Week. A third day is for the school assembly with the production of two plays and a short address by the children's author.

Additional Ways Favorite Books Can Be Shared

- Display illustrated maps showing a character's travels or the area a book encompasses.

- Have students dress as one of the characters in the book and answer questions in an interview or newscast.

- Have students, as book characters, exchange letters— students write letters to one another as the characters might.

- Have students write a diary or log to represent the experiences of a book's main character.

- Construct or have the students construct mobiles consisting either of the major characters from the story or of scenes in the plot.

- Encourage students to make booklets about their favorite authors (including the background of the author and other works he or she has written).

- Have students write a thumbnail review of characters to introduce fellow classmates to people they might enjoy getting to know ("You Meet Such Interesting People in Books").

Enduring Concerns of Reading Teachers

Part

IV

Chapter

6

Working with Parents

The enormous influence that parents have on their children's learning has been highlighted time and again in educational literature (Becher, 1985; Rasinski & Fredericks, 1989). Successful teachers of reading realize this fact and view parents as partners in the learning process, capitalizing on the parents' unique position to help their children become good readers. This team approach, focusing on positive action and growth both in school and at home, has been proven effective (Maring & Magelky, 1990). Vehicles to promote various ways for parents to foster their children's reading abilities have become (and rightfully so) hits with libraries, journals and magazines, professional organizations, parent groups, state departments of education, the U.S. Department of Education, and publishing houses. The ERIC (Educational Resource Information Center) Clearinghouse on Reading and Communication Skills at Indiana University has produced a new audio journal, *Parents and Children Together*. As its name indicates, this new aid is directed toward parents and children, and contains helpful tips to promote literacy. Professional organizations and numerous local sources also can provide many excellent resources, including books, pamphlets, and articles, on this topic. This chapter aims to present practical tips and guidelines for beginning teachers in communicating and working effectively with parents.

PUTTING YOUR TELEPHONE TO WORK

Judiciously used, the telephone provides an excellent line of communication between teacher and parent throughout the school year. Even before the year's first open house, teachers should take the time to call each parent at home during the first week of school to introduce themselves. This creates an atmosphere of togetherness and openness. With a class of twenty to thirty children, this may take three or four evenings, but it starts off the year on a positive note. The parents will be impressed because the teacher took the time to call and individually talk to each one of them. When children come to school the next day, they are usually impressed that their teacher called just to say "hello." This telephone conversation should also be planned and informative. Explain your expectations, homework procedures, projects and how the parent might help you during the year.

Another use of the telephone is as a reward. The teacher can call to tell the parents what a good job their child did on a vocabulary test or a book report or to mention a courtesy the child did for a teacher or another student. Again, parents are usually surprised by telephone calls that share good behavior. In addition to calling in the first week of school, teachers should try to call about all the children during the first semester of the school year. Most telephone conversations with parents are associated

Often a teacher can effectively communicate a child's strengths to his or her parents over the telephone.
Stuart Spates

with negatives, so when parents get a telephone call just to discuss the classroom, they are pleasantly surprised.

Another activity that promotes cooperation between parents and teachers is a "student of the week" program. Each week, the teacher secretly selects a student who has had a good week to be student of the week for the next week. The teacher calls the parents and asks them either to send a picture of their child through a friend or to drop one off at school (without the students' knowing it). Teachers can display these pictures on a classroom bulletin board. This also helps the students develop a good self-concept. Teachers are encouraged to develop other ideas to show off their students and promote good relations with parents.

THE GROUP MEETING: OPEN HOUSE

Teachers and parents will participate together in two types of meetings during the school year: the "open house," or large-group meeting, and the individual parent-teacher conference. Both are important and need to be planned carefully by the teacher. The open house is usually held at the beginning of the school year and introduces the teachers and their programs to the parents. Parents are very curious and want to "examine" the new teacher, so this meeting is usually well-attended. A good proverb for teachers to keep in mind as they plan this session is, "You don't get a second chance to make a first impression." Teachers should remember to smile, relax, and be enthusiastic, since most parents do want to help; they are simply unsure of how to go about it. Parents look to the teachers as the professionals.

Outline for Group Presentation—Open House

1. Teachers should introduce themselves. They should include information on their background, hobbies, family, and why they chose teaching as a career.

2. Teachers should discuss their goals, and those of the school, for the coming year. They should include what they hope to accomplish with each child in the class academically, socially, and emotionally. The teachers should also explain the daily routine and perhaps have the schedule written on the board or a chart.

3. Teachers should discuss the entire academic program and curriculum for the year, emphasizing the role of reading, writing, listening, and speaking as they relate to each subject area.

4. Teachers also need to discuss the reading program and give examples of how the class will be organized. They should list and explain some of the skills and abilities that will be focused on during the year.

5. The variety of approaches that will be incorporated into the reading program should also be explained (for example, the basal text, whole language, literature, individualized instruction, and small-group and large-group approaches).

6. Teachers should emphasize that they will maintain a positive atmosphere in the classroom. Management techniques, teacher expectations, student responsibilities, assignments, and student portfolios can be described.

7. Teachers should explain ways parents can get in touch with them, and that the teachers will be calling on them to help. If planning to send home a monthly newsletter, the teacher should explain its purpose and use. Some teachers send home a survey to ask parents to volunteer to go on field trips, to be a room mother or father, or to make telephone calls. All these ways give parents a feeling of belonging.

8. Teachers should distribute a handout on how parents can help at home with reading. A sample handout is included later in this chapter. Remember, though, don't hand out the material if there is no time to explain the information it contains.

9. Teachers should tell parents how pleased they are to see them at the open house. Remind parents of the tremendous influence they can have on their children's success this coming year.

ONE ON ONE: THE PARENT-TEACHER CONFERENCE

Individual parent conferences have the explicit purpose of giving parents specific information about the progress of their children and are the chief means of communication between parents and teachers. Student teachers should make certain they have an opportunity to sit in on a conference that their sponsoring or cooperating teacher is conducting. Such a conference, to be effective, takes preparation on the teacher's part. Many parents leave the conference disappointed because they have not been given specific information. The professional needs to keep this in mind when planning the conference. Make suggestions that parents can take home and implement easily.

In preparation for the conference, write down some notes concerning each child academically, socially, and emotionally. Examine the student's portfolio and select samples of his or her work. An important detail to consider is the seating arrangement of the actual conference. Use a conference table for an informal arrangement. Stay away from sitting behind the desk, as this gives the impression of an employer-employee relationship. A desk sometimes is a barrier to an open conversation.

A teacher might follow the following sample outline in preparing for a parent conference:

Planning for the Parent-Teacher Conference

1. Welcome the parent or parents to your room. Ask them how their child is enjoying school this year and whether he or she talks about school at home. The first few minutes of the conference should be informal and should set the tone for the meeting. Be a good listener.

2. Inform the parents of their child's progress in reading. Have samples of the child's work available.

3. Discuss both the child's strengths and areas where he or she needs help. Don't forget to emphasize strengths, yet carefully explain areas in which the student needs to improve.

4. Discuss other areas, such as getting along with others, handing work in on time, and other responsibilities. A list of these can usually be found on most school systems' report cards.

5. Discuss specific recommendations on how to handle any school problems. If the problem involves other school professionals, seek out the principal to make the necessary contacts. If parents need to make an appointment with the principal or guidance counselor, see if you can help them schedule it.

6. If the problem is one you can handle, have the specifics available. Be prepared to demonstrate any techniques to the parents. If you are going to give parents a handout, have enough time to explain it and demonstrate how the parents should use it at home with their child. If you say to the parents, "Practice reading with your child," make sure the parents can, and are willing to, do this activity. Be specific; give them a book or suggest one that is on the child's independent or "easy" level. Suggest that the parents read a paragraph, then have the child read a paragraph. Also, provide the parents with questions to ask, such as: "Tell me in your own words what happened in the story. Did you like the story? Do you think that the story really happened? What part did you like the best? What part did you not like? What do you think will happen next?" Be clear and stay away from educational jargon.

7. Conclude the conference by summarizing what you are going to do and what the parents are going to do.

8. Thank the parents for coming, and remind them that by working together you can both help the child to be successful at school.

9. When the conference is over, reflect on the conversation and write down important points and recommendations.

Do's and Don'ts for the Parent-Teacher Conference

Successful face-to-face interaction with parents is an absolute necessity for an effective conference. Packer (1990) has worked extensively in the field of teacher-parent communication. His suggestions, titled "Do's and Don'ts for Parent Conferencing," are helpful for all teachers to follow. They are summarized below:

Do:

1. Keep eye contact.

2. Use positive body language.

3. Use active listening, paraphrasing, perception checking, wait-time.

4. Ask questions.

5. Show concern.

6. Show you are glad the parents came in.

7. Say something positive.

8. Have materials of student available to share, if possible.

9. Avoid comparing with other children.

10. Be cooperative.

11. Show respect.

12. Avoid jargon.

13. Be specific whenever possible.

14. Be honest and direct.

15. Be understanding and flexible.

16. Be patient.

17. Be willing to negotiate and compromise.

18. End on a positive note.

19. Be understanding of the other person's point of view.

20. Be glad that parents' feelings are brought to your attention.

21. Set the stage for the conference—establish the reason for meeting.

22. Be clear about why you do what you do.

23. Give appropriate compliments.

24. Try to make clear statements.

25. Be supportive and strong.

Don't:

1. Interrupt or cut the parents off.

2. Lose self-control.

3. Argue with the parents.

4. Insinuate that parents are the cause of any problems.

5. Get defensive.

6. Compare the child with others or leave the parents "hanging."

7. Be close-minded.

8. Get angry.

9. Be stubborn.

10. Go totally against the parent (don't act as an adversary).

11. Say something just to please the parent.*

Handout: How to Help Your Child at Home

It is helpful for teachers to have practical suggestions that promote effective communication and involvement with parents. On page 151 is a suggested handout that teachers can give to parents to make specific suggestions on how they can help at home with reading. The handout can be explained during the individual conference. A suggestion would be to develop other handouts in other areas that could be used in the same way. Again, be advised that these handouts are of little value unless the teachers explain them.

OTHER SUGGESTIONS FOR PARENT-TEACHER COOPERATION

Ideally, if all parents cooperated and participated in their children's education, students and teachers would benefit immensely. However, we realize many pressures and realities in today's society inhibit parents from participating fully in school activities. Given the realities of poverty, the changing nature of the American family, the high student mobility common in many schools across the nation, and our culturally pluralistic society, teachers need to be sensitive to student and parent needs and desires. Teachers must strive to involve parents in their children's education in creative and nontraditional ways. The following are additional suggestions to help involve parents in school activities:

- Visit parents. You may wish to bring a non-threatening person, such as a retired person or a minister, with you,

- Send home a weekly or bimonthly newsletter summarizing school happenings. For parents whose primary

* Packer, A. (1990). *Parent Involvement/Interpersonal Communications.* Packet of readings. Gainesville, FL: 56.

HOW TO HELP YOUR CHILD AT HOME

I. The Home
  A. Become a reading and writing family.
  B. Discuss daily experiences with your child and listen to what he or she has to say.
  C. Set aside some time each day for reading.
  D. Spend your reading time with your child in a quiet room.
  E. Do not deprive the child of television or outdoor playtime to read with him or her.
  F. Give books and magazine subscriptions as gifts.
  G. Set up a home library.
  H. Foster positive attitudes toward reading and writing.

II. Materials
  A. School library books.
  B. Public library books.
  C. Children's paperback books at, for example, mall bookstores.
  D. Newspapers and magazines.

III. Methods
  A. Let the child select his or her own library book or magazine. Never tell your child that the book is too easy.
  B. Encourage the development of interests. What the child is interested in reading, he or she will enjoy.
  C. Read aloud to your child every day. At times, write and illustrate a story together.
  D. Tell your child words he or she does not know. Do not say, "That's an easy word," or "You've had that word before."
  E. Discuss a book your child is reading, asking for a summary or for a comparison with the last book read.
  F. Encourage your child by reading yourself and discussing your stories.
  G. Do not read an entire article orally. Select a funny part—a surprising part—a favorite part.
  H. Help increase your child's listening, speaking, and reading vocabulary by discussing various words and by beginning a collection of new words. Also, play various vocabulary games to reinforce new words.
  I. Praise your child for a job well done.

IV. Help
  A. Don't spend a lot of time trying to get your child to pronounce words correctly; make reading at home a pleasant, positive experience for all concerned.
  B. Ask the teacher for some suggestions for word games if your child needs help in specific areas.
  C. Don't hesitate to call the teacher if you need help or don't understand something. Working as a team, you will help your child learn to read.

V. Finally, the only way to learn to read is to *read,* and then to *discuss* what you read with someone. Encourage your child to read newspapers, magazines, and quality literature, and talk about them together.

language is not English, write the letter in their native language.

- For parents who can spare an hour or two a week, design a volunteer program so they can come to the classroom and help in some way. Acknowledge their contribution in the newsletter.

- Provide transportation and baby-sitting help for parents to come to parent-teacher conferences at the school. Often various social agencies will provide transportation, and high school students can baby-sit while parents attend school functions.

- Arrange parent-teacher conferences in a neighborhood center or church.

SUMMARY

The ability of teachers and parents to work together as partners in the teaching-learning process is crucial to each child's success in reading. Unfortunately, most teachers receive little instruction in effective parent communications and ways to promote parental involvement in classroom and school activities. In this chapter, we presented specific guidelines for teachers to work with parents. We discussed practical suggestions for having a successful beginning-of-the-year open-house meeting and individual parent-teacher conferences throughout the year. The importance of contacting parents by telephone was stressed, especially to focus on positive happenings in the class. Effective teachers not only encourage parents to become involved with their children's education but also take the time to show parents exactly what to do. To keep abreast of innovative ideas and programs to increase parent involvement, teachers need to participate in professional organizations and read the professional literature.

Discussion Questions and Student Projects: Working with Parents

1. Even though it is widely publicized that parents need to be involved in school activities, many parents are not involved in their children's education and do not visit schools. Why not? What do you plan to do to increase parent participation when you teach?

2. Role-play two parent-teacher conferences dealing with students experiencing difficulty in reading: one conference with parents who feel comfortable in your classroom, having volunteered in classrooms in previous years, and another conference with parents who feel very uncomfortable in your classroom and who have rarely visited schools or communicated with teachers. Discuss feelings of all persons involved and brainstorm corrective measures to be taken in each conference. If possible, videotape each conference and critique each one with your peers. What additional strategies and expertise are needed to be successful

in dealing with parents who feel uncomfortable in a parent-teacher conference?

3. Programs using parents as tutors are proliferating across the nation. Read a journal article describing one such program and summarize it for your peers.

Chapter
7

Selecting
Reading Materials

One major challenge today's teachers face is selecting appropriate instructional materials. The large quantity available only adds to that challenge. With this abundance comes the requirement that teachers develop the ability to evaluate the materials in terms of quality and to determine which ones will best meet both the curricular goals for the complete reading program, and individual students' differences and needs. Because such a broad range of attractive materials is available, it is easy to place a disproportionate emphasis on their use. Although the choice and appropriate use of materials directly affect the students' success in reading, the most significant factor in determining student achievement in reading remains the teacher.

Typical materials usually available in most classrooms include (1) a commercial reading program (either a literature-based program or a basal reader program that includes student readers; workbooks; teacher's manuals; placement, pre-unit, and post-unit tests; visual aids; and flash cards, games, and computer software); (2) materials to supplement the program (books, kits, games, worksheets, and computer software); (3) children's literature; and (4) teacher-made materials (Heilman, Blair, & Rupley, 1990). Teachers are expected to know how to use such materials within the framework of the complete reading program.

THE COMPLETE READING PROGRAM: INSTRUCTIONAL, CONTENT, RECREATIONAL, CORRECTIVE

Effective material selection should be guided by the four major components of the complete reading program. A brief review of those components, along with the different types of materials appropriate to each, is given below.

In the *instructional* reading component, the basic reading skills of word identification, vocabulary, and comprehension are taught. Materials that reinforce, or provide practice in using, the same skills presented in the lesson are considered most effective. Because a high rate of success enhances student learning, materials should cover only those skills previously taught. Teachers should avoid using materials that contain irrelevant skills or any new skills that would be prerequisite to the completion of the task because such skills would be too difficult to learn, and the result would be frustration and failure. Practice materials also need to be structured and sequenced, with the skill being broken down into small, closely related steps to maximize learning. Language experience, literature-based, and basal programs are the primary materials used in instructional reading.

In the *content* reading component, students receive systematic instruction on both specific strategies for studying content area texts and the skills necessary to comprehend expository text. Materials for this component include content-area texts, maps, charts, graphs, diagrams, tables, card catalogs, dictionaries, encyclopedias, almanacs, atlases, and other reference books. This component can also teach students how to apply reading skills to obtain practical information necessary for real-life situations. Materials such as newspapers, telephone directories, catalogs, driver's manuals, job and loan applications, and train, bus, and airplane schedules are often used.

Teachers provide students with the opportunity to apply their reading skills and increase their knowledge in a variety of areas in the *recreational* reading component. For this component students usually independently read books of their own choosing, most often library books and paperbacks of various types of literature but sometimes newspapers and magazines. Often this component is accomplished by incorporating USSR (Uninterrupted Sustained Silent Reading), because research indicates that this method helps improve abilities in recreational reading. It is also believed to improve students' attitudes and to encourage lifelong reading habits.

The *corrective* component is designed to help students practice strategies and skills not yet mastered. For mastery to be achieved, these strategies and skills need to be transferred to real reading situations. In order for transfer to occur, reading skills and strategies must be practiced in a variety of situations. Appropriate materials for this component usually include high-interest low-vocabulary readers, supplemental readers, reading games and kits, software, audiovisual aids, workbooks, dittos, teacher-made materials, newspapers, and magazines.

CHOOSING INSTRUCTIONAL MATERIAL

Teacher-Effectiveness Literature

A review of the teacher-effectiveness literature can provide helpful guidelines for choosing appropriate instructional materials. The literature on teaching indicates that effective teachers target student needs and program goals in selecting and using a variety of materials. Additional concerns include the actual content of the materials, the promotion of time spent on academics, and student interest.

Content of Reading Materials

The content covered in instructional materials is one of the most important factors for teachers to consider in choosing materials. When teachers are planning instruction and selecting materials, they must first accurately diagnose individual needs. Only then should they determine instructional goals and types of materials. For optimum learning to occur, teachers must make the goals of instruction clear to the students. Materials that contain clearly stated objectives and those with clear directions are most beneficial. When determining instructional goals, it is helpful to select materials that cover skills and strategies congruent with reading skill development. One key question teachers should ask themselves is whether the material will help the student to become an independent reader. If the answer is "no," teachers need to reevaluate why they have chosen that material.

Teachers also need to make sure the materials have content validity; that is, that they really cover what the guides indicate they cover. It is not uncommon for worksheets to lack content validity. For example, a worksheet reviewing the final *e* principle may require students to circle words that have a silent *e*. In such a case, students do not necessarily have to read the words. They may successfully complete the task merely by identifying those words containing two vowels, the latter of which is the letter *e*. A worksheet of this type is primarily a visual discrimination task and does not help reinforce true reading skills. In *The Report of the Commission on Reading*, Anderson et al. (1985) state, "Students frequently don't read all the material in worksheets. Instead, they attempt to use shortcuts that allow them to answer in a mechanical fashion" (p. 75). Whether the teacher uses worksheets, kits, computer games, or other aids, it is essential that he or she check the content validity of the material to be certain the skill is being applied in a real reading situation.

The content of all materials should reflect sound pedagogy. Teachers will want to ask themselves if the content is based on current research. Is the material being used primarily because of its motivational quality, or is there research to support the effectiveness of its use?

Examining the content covered, content validity, and the pedagogical basis of the content are all essential parts of choosing materials appropriate for each component of the complete reading program.

Academic Learning Time

Another essential component of choosing instructional materials is academic learning time. Academic learning time consists of three basic components: (1) allocated time; (2) engaged time; and (3) student success rate (Fisher, Marliave, & Filby, 1979). Allocated time refers to the amount of time assigned for covering or mastering the content. It is positively related to student achievement. Engaged time refers to the amount of time during which students are actively involved in the lesson. Any form of information processing—such as reading, thinking, interacting with worksheets, kits, workbooks, and learning centers, manipulating objects, or academic interaction with other students—constitutes active engagement. Student success rate refers to the level of difficulty of the given task. If the task is at an appropriate level of difficulty and the students are able to produce many correct responses, they are more likely to be learning. Thus, academic learning time refers to the amount of time students are successfully engaged in an appropriate academic task. When teachers increase academic learning time, the result tends to be greater reading achievement (Anderson, Evertson, & Brophy, 1979). Academic learning time can be enhanced through the appropriate selection of materials. Effective instructional materials should increase engaged time, student success rate, and allocated time.

Student Interest

To increase engaged time, the time students are actively involved in learning a skill, the students must be interested in the material. One effective way to capture students' interest is by making sure the material contains diverse activities. Varied instructional materials may include games (word games, board games, and computer games, among others), puppets, tapes, records, filmstrips, videos, interactive video, compact disk read-only memories (CD ROMs), or worksheets. Although all instructional materials cannot be as motivating as interactive video and computer games, teachers can select a variety of materials that capture students' interests. Worksheets can be interesting, depending on the content, level of difficulty, requirement of different types of tasks (such as writing, marking, coloring, cutting, and pasting), and visual appeal (including the placement of pictures, how current the pictures are, the use of color, and the type, size, and style of the print). Thus, a varied format within the materials helps to motivate students. Perhaps the best way for a teacher to determine whether the material will motivate students is to ask himself or herself, "If I were placed in the student's position, would I have enough interest to complete the assignment?"

Allocated time may be enhanced by choosing materials that ensure students have sufficient time to practice and master the lesson content. Since allocated time contributes to increased academic learning time, teachers need to determine whether the time spent completing instructional materials will indeed contribute to the students' mastery of the content. Teachers also need to consider how much of the instructional material requires actual reading and how much requires activities outside reading, such as writing, circling, and coloring. According to *The Report of the Commission on Reading* (Anderson et al., 1985):

Analyses of workbook activities reveal that many require only a perfunctory level of reading. . . . Few activities foster fluency, or constructive and strategic reading. . . . Instead, responses usually involve filling a word in a blank, circling or underlining an item, or selecting one of several choices. Many workbook exercises drill students on skills that have little value in learning to read (pp. 74–75).

Since students spend up to 70 percent of their reading instruction time on worksheets (Anderson et al., 1985), making sure the activities provide the opportunity to master the skill in a real reading situation is imperative. The skill that is practiced is the skill that is learned. Therefore, the major concern should be that the students receive sufficient practice applying the skill in actual reading situations.

Student success rate can be increased by choosing materials that match the students' ability level. Such materials allow the students to make many correct responses and therefore result in a high success rate. A high success rate is generally defined as tasks that are completed with a minimum of 80 percent accuracy. Teachers need to avoid using materials with tasks so difficult that few correct responses are made. To increase the amount of student learning, there must be a match between the level of the material and the ability level of the students.

By selecting appropriate materials that enhance academic learning time, teachers help develop the success of the instructional, corrective, and content components of the complete reading program.

SELECTING LITERATURE

Regardless of the type of reading program selected, literature is an essential component of the complete reading program. Huck, Hepler, and Hickman (1979) estimate that children will read approximately 25 books a year, totaling some 200 books during their childhood. They also state, "With over 40,000 children's books in print, it is possible that a child may read widely, yet never read a significant book" (p. 33). Although the reasons for, and the values of, using literature in the complete reading program are voluminous, the focus of this section of the chapter is to help teachers know how to choose appropriate literature.

As a result of the current movement toward literature-based programs, some states now provide handbooks and recommended reading lists for their teachers. For example, the state of California has devoted several publications to the area of reading/language arts alone, including the *Handbook for Planning an Effective Literature Program* and *Annotated Recommended Readings in Literature* (one for kindergarten through grade eight, and one for grades nine through twelve). The kindergarten through grade eight list contains approximately 1,000 book titles, is annotated, identifies literary contributions of specific ethnic or cultural groups, and provides a range of grade levels for which each book may be appropriate. These recommended lists are available by writing to the California State Department of Education, P.O. Box 271, Sacramento, CA 95802-0271. Although such guidelines are helpful, not all states provide recommended lists. In any case, teachers need to know how to choose literature appropriate for their own classrooms.

To competently select literature, teachers need to be well-read themselves, knowledgeable of what constitutes literary quality, perceptive regarding the backgrounds and development of their students, and well-informed about instructional strategies that will both teach literature and motivate students to read literature independently. Some major factors influencing teachers' selections are literary value, children's interests, and individual reading ability.

Literary Value

One way to select literature is to examine the literary elements of plot, characterization, setting, theme, style, and point of view. The following discussion, based on Norton (1991), provides a brief overview of each element. A good plot usually consists of action, excitement, some suspense, and conflict. It allows students to become involved in the action, feel the conflict developing, recognize the climax, and develop and sustain interest. Quality characterization needs to develop believable characters with families, pasts, futures, hopes, fears, sorrows, and happiness. The characters should be realistic, revealing their true nature, strengths and weaknesses alike. A good setting provides details that reinforce both the plot and characterization. The theme should tie the plot, characterization, and setting together. Books that have worthwhile themes are those that students can understand because the themes relate to the students' needs. The style helps create the plot, characterization, setting, and theme; therefore, the style should mirror the setting of the story and the background of the characters. One way to determine the quality of style is through oral reading. The language should appeal to the senses, bring the characters to life, enhance the plot development, and create the mood. Jim Trelease's *New Read-Aloud Handbook* (1989) is an excellent source that includes lists of books that lend themselves to oral reading. In evaluating the point of view, regardless of which point of view the author chose (first person, objective, omniscient, or limited omniscient), teachers should examine how well the choice influenced the other literary elements.

Children's Interests

Another means for selecting appropriate literature is to consider the children's interests. The major goals of every reading teacher are to foster a love and appreciation for literature and to develop lifelong reading habits. The Children's Book Council, along with the International Reading Association, recognizes the importance of students' interests and compiles a list of "Children's Choices" published in each October issue of *The Reading Teacher.* Turner (1989) states, "[C]hildren rarely read good literature if they have not been exposed to books that interest them and that are popular among their peers" (p. 16). Children's interest can easily be determined through administering and evaluating interest inventories. Perhaps the easiest way to discover children's interests is through informal conversations. In the classroom, some type of record-keeping is necessary to match individual interests with appropriate books.

Reading Ability

Appropriate literature for the classroom cannot be selected on literary quality and children's interests alone. The students' reading ability is a major factor in literature selection. In order for students to develop both a love of literature and lifelong reading habits, they must be able to experience success when reading independently. This does not mean that books with a challenging vocabulary should be avoided. According to Schmidtmann (1989):

> Children love words that give them a hard time, provided they are in a context that absorbs their attention. Consider . . . [E.B. White's *Charlotte's Web*]. Charlotte certainly makes learning

vocabulary fun. Her dialogues with Wilber are filled with such words as 'salutations,' 'untenable,' 'aeronaut,' and 'sedentary.' Hardly the vocabulary for an 8-year-old, but with Charlotte explaining them, children see the words in context, and feel satisfied that they have improved their reading (p. 210).

When selecting literature, the key is to match the student and the book, according to both interest and reading ability.

Additional Considerations

Two other factors affecting teachers' book selection are the content and the availability and/or accessibility of literature. Teachers should review the content of the books in terms of appropriateness to the students' level of emotional and intellectual maturity. The way in which authors deal with sensitive issues will also help the teachers determine the appropriateness of the content.

On a practical level, availability and accessibility will affect the choices teachers and students make. Given the limited budget within which most teachers must work, they are compelled to use only those books the district or community libraries offer. Other sources may be available, however. Some community libraries will send boxes of books to the classroom on a regular basis. Teachers may indicate specific topics or allow the librarian to make the choice. One effective and inexpensive way to increase the number of available books is to seek help from colleagues teaching higher grade levels. They can ask their students' parents to donate children's books that they are no longer using. Another way to collect books is through the local libraries. Every year libraries "clean their shelves" by giving books away or by selling them at very reasonable rates. Money from small fund-raising projects, such as bake sales or white elephant sales, can be used to purchase these valuable but inexpensive books. If teachers want students to learn to love literature, it is the teachers' responsibility to make sure a wide variety of literature is easily accessible. The greater the opportunity to read, the more reading will occur.

Last, the literature available must be balanced. Selections should contain an appropriate mix of classic and contemporary literature from as many different genres as possible, including folktales, fables, myths, fantasy, poetry, realistic and historical fiction, biography, autobiography, and informational books. Ideally the books should also have an equal representation of females and minorities in central and leadership roles. When making selections, teachers also need to provide a wide variety of multicultural books. Books that cover many different cultural and ethnic topics are crucial. Providing students with the opportunity to read about others from different racial, religious, and ethnic backgrounds allows them to go beyond their own lives and gain insight into the lives of others. Such books allow students to experience vicariously and to understand the many dimensions of our society.

COMPUTER SOFTWARE

As is the case with any other material selection, the effectiveness of computer software selection depends not only on the software being used but also on how well teachers match the software programs with individual student needs.

The computer can be an effective tool in teaching reading.
Stuart Spates

Software Programs

Software programs usually consist of drill and practice, tutorial dialogues, simulations, and learning games and may include telecommunications. Of the different types of programs, a majority fall into the drill and practice category. Drill and practice programs usually present practice exercises on specific skills, require a student response, and are followed by a computer response. The computer response provides feedback about whether students have answered correctly. Some drill and practice programs have record-keeping capabilities that allow the teachers to monitor students' progress. Some programs also allow the teachers to control the pace of the drill. The programs are written based on the assumption that the teachers have already introduced the basic skill. The intent of the programs is to enable students to practice skills independently until they achieve mastery. Drill and practice programs can be particularly helpful for the instructional component of the complete reading program and can be easily incorporated into the independent practice portion of the direct instruction lesson.

Tutorial dialogues provide practice exercises, but they also offer instruction through explanations. They are based on the assumption that the students may have had little or no instruction on the skill covered. Tutorial dialogues also have branching capabilities. Instead of strictly providing practice exercises, they are designed to reroute the students according to their skill level. For example, if students give many incorrect responses, the program cycles back and reviews an explanation of the skill, then provides more practice exercises. If, conversely, students give many correct responses, the program branches to a more difficult level of material. The availability of tutorial dialogue programs is somewhat limited because of the expense of the programming involved. However, they can be very helpful in the corrective component of the complete reading program, especially during the reteaching step of the direct reading lesson.

Simulation programs allow students to role-play in some lifelike situation that requires decision making about complex events. In this type of program, the computer presents an experiment or a hypothetical situation that requires the students to solve a problem. As the students respond and progress through the program, the computer gives additional information and displays current results of the decision the students made. According to Balajthy (1986), the use of computer simulations has several advantages. They can give students experiences that may be impractical for the teacher to provide, such as dangerous or expensive experiments or field trips to faraway places, or they may present experiences that are impossible for students actually to have, such as simulating some event of the past. Simulations are thought to help develop background knowledge and analytical thinking. They are easily incorporated into the classroom and are considered to be very motivating.

Learning games offer students interesting and varied practice in different learning skills. Although the validity of their use has been questioned, they are popular because most students find them highly motivating. With careful selections, teachers can provide games designed to reinforce skill development. These games can be used to support the instructional or the recreational component of the complete reading program. They also can be useful during the independent practice portion of a direct instruction lesson.

Telecommunication programs allow students to communicate with others outside their immediate environment via the use of a modem. A modem is a device that enables computers to communicate over telephone lines. In order to communicate long distances with the computer, a network must be in place. Simply stated, a network is a set of microcomputers connected so that messages can be sent and received between one place and another. One component of telecommunications is electronic mail or bulletin boards. Instead of communicating directly over the telephone, students can write messages on the computer and send them electronically through the modem to others. Although the use of telecommunications and electronic mail is only beginning to appear in school settings, there are positive implications for its potential in promoting the reading-writing connection.

It would be wonderful if school budgets were as abundant as the materials. The reality, however, is that some teachers do not even get enough paper to run off dittos. How then would they ever get modems and phone lines in their classrooms? A wide selection of computers, software, modems, VCRs, CD ROMs, and interactive videos are all available through outside funding. Most school administrators either are familiar with grants designed specifically for classroom teachers or can lead teachers to the appropriate sources. Any teachers who can write and are willing to take the time to apply for a grant can have all the imagined technology at their fingertips.

To choose appropriate software programs, whether for drill and practice, tutorial dialogues, simulations, learning games, or telecommunications, an excellent reference is Strickland, Feeley, and Wepner's (1987) *Using Computers in the Teaching of Reading.* The authors describe many software programs they feel beneficial specifically for classroom reading teachers.

Evaluating Software

To make effective software choices appropriate for use in the classroom, it is important to know how to evaluate programs. When evaluating software, teachers should examine all the same components that are involved in evaluating any other instructional material. Additional evaluation considerations specific to computer software fall under the categories of instructional design, ease of use, and record-keeping.

Hofmeister (1984) offers the following guidelines for evaluating the instructional design of software. When examining the instructional design, teachers will want to decide the importance of each of the following items and be aware of whether the program:

- Allows the rate and sequence of instruction to be controlled.
- Can be used independently.
- Allows learners to interact only with appropriate segments.
- Uses a variety of display and response modes.
- Minimizes typing.
- Handles a wide range of student responses appropriately.
- Provides summaries and reviews or restates important concepts.
- Can be adapted to individual needs.
- Uses appropriate graphics, color, and sound.
- Provides appropriate, immediate, and varied feedback.
- Allows active rather than passive interaction.
- Uses displays that are clear, understandable, and effective.

- Provides a sufficient number of practice exercises.

- Is an appropriate length.

- Generates further assignments.

- Has branching capabilities.

- Has record-keeping capabilities (pp. 7–10).

Determining the ease of use involves examining the type and amount of "help" procedures available. It is also prudent to find out how easily students can enter and exit the program. The documentation that comes with the software provides a hard copy of all the instructions and therefore is valuable in determining the ease of use. One of the most effective ways to evaluate the ease of use is for teachers to try the program themselves.

For those programs that contain record-keeping systems, teachers will want to decide whether the guidelines presented below will meet their individual needs. Teachers may want to consider whether the program:

- Keeps accurate records of student responses.

- Keeps ongoing student records.

- Graphically depicts student progress.

- Provides statistical information on student progress.

- Allows a printout and screen display of student records.

- Includes diagnostic/evaluative testing (Hofmeister, 1984, pp. 7–11).

Aside from using the above criteria for software evaluation, teachers can enlist the aid of their students. Since students will be required to spend their time using the programs, and oftentimes tend to be more computer literate than many adults, their feedback can be invaluable. Another helpful source for evaluating software is the reviews published in educational magazines.

TEACHER-MADE MATERIALS

Despite the tremendous amount of commercial reading materials available, publishers simply cannot cover the broad range of instructional needs, nor are they able to design material appropriate for the unique needs of each student. To meet the instructional demands of their classrooms, most teachers have recognized and acted upon the need to make their own materials.

Teacher-made materials are a very important part of teacher effectiveness. If the materials address student needs, learning is enhanced. The students are usually more motivated, and more likely to stay involved, when materials match both interests and needs. Learning can also increase when teachers allow the students to become involved in making reading materials. One exciting aspect of teacher-made materials is that the kind of materials teachers devise is limited only by their imagination. Every area of reading, whether it is word identification, comprehension, vocabulary, or study skills, permits the use of teacher-made materials. Often teachers will come across materials that have excellent ideas, but either the material is too expensive or the levels and/or the skills covered are inappropriate for the students' needs. A common way to make materials is to use the best ideas presented in existing materials and adapt them to specific needs.

SUMMARY

Today's teachers of reading have a wide variety of instructional materials available to them, ranging from commercial reading programs to supplemental materials (such as kits, games, worksheets, dittos, and computer software), to a variety of children's literature. Effective teachers examine all the components of a complete reading program and choose materials that will support each component and match the students' instructional needs. When selecting materials, one of the most important questions teachers can ask is whether the materials will indeed serve to develop independent readers who can both understand the printed message and strategically monitor their own reading comprehension (Principle 4). Given the plethora of materials available, the ability to select those appropriate for reading instruction is essential to effective teaching. To choose wisely, teachers must be knowledgeable, but must also recognize their own importance. It is the teacher who ultimately determines students' success or failure in learning to read.

Discussion Questions and Student Projects: Selecting Reading Materials

1. To what degree do you think the selection of instructional materials influences teacher effectiveness?

2. What might be some additional ways to increase the availability of instructional materials? What might you do to improve your existing instructional materials?

3. Aside from books, are any instructional materials an absolute necessity for the successful teaching of reading? If so, what? If not, why not?

4. Design and produce six self-correcting games and activities in the area of word identification.

5. Conduct an ERIC search in the library for recent publications regarding (a) literature-based reading approaches; (b) language experience approach; (c) whole-language programs; and (d) basal reader programs. Write a summary of one article dealing with each of these approaches.

Chapter
8

Growing in Your Profession

The responsibility to help students become successful in reading is a shared responsibility, with the teacher playing a fundamental role in the process. The importance of the classroom teacher of reading has been emphasized on many occasions as a key factor in whether students succeed in mastering one of the most crucial communication abilities—reading. This text has aimed to synthesize new knowledge about the teaching of reading in a form usable by teachers, to present actual examples of essential lessons teachers are expected to perform, and to help foster a self-monitoring or reflective attitude toward teaching. These important purposes are never finished. Effective teachers at any level in any subject are characterized as learners. If teachers stagnate and do not grow and continually develop as professionals, their enthusiasm will ultimately suffer. Just as effective medical doctors must keep abreast of new knowledge and techniques to treat their patients, and must continually monitor their own effectiveness, so, too, must effective teachers keep abreast of new knowledge and techniques and monitor their effectiveness in the classroom.

Speaking of the importance of quality in teaching, Corrigan (1982) listed several principles as conditions for improving our schools and teacher education. The following principle speaks directly to the importance of being a knowledgeable professional:

Teaching is a matter of life and death. The tragedy is that most people do not recognize the life-and-death nature of teaching. Every moment in the lives of teachers and pupils brings critical decisions of motivation, reinforcement, reward, ego enhancement, and goal direction. Proper professional decisions enhance learning and life; improper decisions send the learner towards incremental death in openness to experience and in ability to learn and contribute to society. From this perspective, doctors and lawyers have neither more nor less to do with life and death than do teachers. Indeed, if we do not prepare quality teachers we are not going to have quality doctors or lawyers, or, for that matter, quality engineers or musicians. Because teaching is a matter of life and death, it must be entrusted only to the most thoroughly prepared professionals (p. 2).

Underlying teachers' efforts to continue to grow professionally is the importance of maintaining enthusiasm and excitement for teaching and learning and of sharing this excitement with students. After all, teachers do not enter the profession to reap huge financial gains. Rather, teachers are motivated by their enthusiasm and love of teaching and learning and by the profound influence they can have on each and every student.

How do teachers "keep the home fires burning" in teaching reading, feel good about their contribution and the job they are doing, and continue to grow professionally? This question has been of great interest to educational researchers and school practitioners alike. The organization of the school, conditions of the workplace, and decision-making opportunities for teachers have much to do with it, but what can individual teachers do to enhance their professional growth? Teachers can continue to learn and refine skills by doing the following three things:

1. Communicate with school and community personnel.

2. Participate in professional organizations and read the professional literature.

3. Assess and monitor their own teaching and program effectiveness.

COMMUNICATING WITH SCHOOL AND COMMUNITY PERSONNEL

To continue to grow as professionals, teachers can first make a concerted effort to develop a dialogue with other school professionals and, most important, with other members of the community. Effective teachers do not operate in isolation but endeavor to learn as much as they can about their students and consult with several interested parties—other classroom teachers, administrators, supervisors, specialized teachers, librarians, community leaders, representatives of service and volunteer organizations, directors of federal programs, and, especially, parents—to provide the best instruction for their students. In education, we do not have pat answers to all concerns and dilemmas of teaching. Teachers need to share their expertise and learn from the expertise of others to do the best job they can. Without being good listeners and gaining valuable information from key resources both inside and outside the school, teachers will not fully identify and meet students' needs.

To be effective, teachers need to capitalize on their students' backgrounds and interests. Just as a schema theory proposes that readers should capitalize on experience to foster meaningful interaction, effective teacher-student relationships are dependent upon teachers knowing the world of their students. Students spend only approximately six hours a day in school. It is imperative to realize that students are affected by their home background and by the community in which they live. In actuality, all students bring their home background and community values with them to the classroom every day. In addition to both communicating with school personnel to gain valuable information to help students and being cognizant of students' backgrounds and interests, teachers need to be proactive in building partnerships with parents and community personnel. One excellent way to do this is to utilize parents and community resources to enhance the reading program. Teachers can visit town libraries, city buildings, museums, art galleries, parks, and businesses to motivate students and to gain ideas for topics for various reading and writing activities. Also, people from these community resources can share their experiences and knowledge with students. All communities have interesting people—citizens of foreign countries, senior citizens with special talents, people who have traveled extensively, professionals in various fields, representatives of local industries and community groups, and individuals with unusual hobbies—who would be honored to come to schools and share information with classes. Every community has untapped resources to enhance the instructional program.

The effective reading teacher gladly draws on the expertise of other professionals, and on the talents and resources of community leaders, to form partnerships for the benefit of a community's students.
Barbara Schaudt

KEEPING UP THROUGH PROFESSIONAL ORGANIZATIONS AND LITERATURE

Teachers can continue to grow and keep up-to-date by joining and participating in various professional organizations and by reading professional journals, magazines, newsletters, and books. Among the many professional associations to consider are general education associations covering all aspects of teaching, including reading/language arts, and organizations for the various subject areas. The two large general organizations in education are the National Education Association (NEA) and the American Federation of Teachers (AFT). The most popular specific organizations for reading/language arts teachers are the International Reading Association (IRA) and the National Council of Teachers of English (NCTE). Most organizations have local, state, and national professional meetings throughout the year with excellent speakers and a display of new resources for teaching reading. There are also a multitude of ways to become involved in the various associations, and presenting papers at professional meetings is one of the best. Each professional association has an abundance of published resources on everything from summaries of new theoretical viewpoints on the reading process to explanations of new reading techniques and teaching strategies to descriptions of successful reading programs to reviews of new reading materials to new and creative reading/language arts materials themselves to be used in the classroom. Not only are professional organizations excellent sources for receiving information on how to improve reading instruction but also they are a way to develop personal contacts with other professionals in the reading profession. The following are some of the major professional organizations and sources for journals and professional materials in the reading/language arts areas.

International Reading Association (IRA)

The IRA publishes journals including *The Reading Teacher*, which emphasizes elementary grades; *Journal of Reading*, which emphasizes secondary, college, and adult reading education; *Reading Research Quarterly*, which publishes significant studies in reading; and *Lectura y Vida*, which covers reading and related studies in the Spanish language. The IRA also publishes a monthly newsletter, *Reading Today*; a Reading Aids Series of paperback books on timely topics; and pamphlets on various practical topics. Additionally, many states have an IRA affiliate journal. The IRA can be reached at 800 Barksdale Road, Newark, Delaware 19711.

National Council of Teachers of English (NCTE)

Among the journals the National Council of Teachers of English publishes are *Language Arts*, emphasizing the elementary grades, and *English Journal*, emphasizing secondary education. At the college level, the NCTE publishes *Teaching English in the Two-Year College*, for community colleges; *College English*, for college professors of English; *College Composition and Communication*, featuring articles on composition for university professors; and *English Education*, featuring articles on various aspects of curriculum and other approaches for professors preparing teachers of English. *Research in the Teaching of English* is a journal featuring research studies on that topic. Like the IRA, the NCTE publishes a monthly newsletter (*NCTE Plus*), as well as various paperback books on timely topics. Many states also have an NCTE affiliate journal. The NCTE can be reached at 1111 Kenyon Road, Urbana, Illinois 61801.

Educational Resource Information Center/Clearinghouse on Reading and Communication Skills (ERIC/RCS)

The ERIC Clearinghouse on Reading and Communication Skills aims to keep educators informed about current developments in education. It is excellent for a variety of professional resources. Among these are materials of new classroom reading and language arts techniques, teaching units, news about successful projects, bibliographies on specific educational topics, speeches, conference proceedings, research findings, and articles on effective practices. The ERIC Clearinghouse on Reading and Communication Skills can be reached at Indiana University, 2805 East 10th Street, Suite 150, Bloomington, Indiana 47408.

ASSESSING AND MONITORING TEACHING AND PROGRAM EFFECTIVENESS

Knowledge of specific skills, instructional techniques, and materials is essential for teachers of reading. However, more important is the teachers' ability to critically analyze their own programs and make adjustments when necessary to ensure that students are receiving instruction based on their needs. Teachers can evaluate their own teaching through a variety of means: audiotaping lessons, videotaping lessons, peer observation of specific aspects of teaching (such as cognitive level of comprehension questions used in discussions, the number of students participating in a lesson, the manner in which different parts of a lesson were covered, and analysis of student time-on-task), and self-monitoring their effectiveness using various rating scales. The eighteen principles presented in the second part of the text serve as a guide to elements of effective teaching in the reading area. Teachers of reading who exert more effort in these selected areas, as delineated in the eighteen principles, can have more confidence that their efforts will result in student learning. Keeping abreast of new knowledge in the reading field and being receptive to making changes in a teaching program based on student needs are benchmarks of professional growth and interest. As a means of looking at themselves and their programs, teachers can turn the eighteen principles into a checklist to informally provide a profile or snapshot of the emphases in a reading program. The following checklist is a means to monitor your own teaching and/or to determine emphases in your field observations. Remember, this is not a means of evaluation, but a process to think about reading instruction and to identify areas where modifications might be made.

Planning Instruction

To what extent does your reading program exhibit each of the following?

	Sufficiently Covered	Needs Improvement
1. Reading activities are integrated with those of the other language arts.	_____	_____
2. Plans are made for a wide range of differences.	_____	_____
3. High expectations are communicated to students and hard work is expected of all students.	_____	_____
4. The overall goal is development of active, strategic readers who understand text.	_____	_____
5. A variety of approaches is used to teach reading.	_____	_____
6. A variety of word identification strategies is taught to students.	_____	_____
7. Positive student attitudes and feelings are cultivated.	_____	_____

	Sufficiently Covered	Needs Improvement
8. Diagnosis is related to instruction.	_____	_____
9. Specialized techniques are employed with students who speak a nonstandard dialect and/or a native language other than English.	_____	_____
10. A team approach is used to plan the students' instructional program.	_____	_____

Teaching Reading

To what extent does your reading program exhibit each of the following?

	Sufficiently Covered	Needs Improvement
11. Instructional strategy or routine to teach a story.	_____	_____
12. Direct model of instruction for teaching specific reading skills, abilities, and strategies.	_____	_____
13. Learning experiences to promote critical thinking through reading and writing.	_____	_____
14. Specific teaching of content reading.	_____	_____
15. Development of recreational reading.	_____	_____

	Sufficiently Covered	Needs Improvement
16. Use of continuous diagnosis to accompany instructional programs.	_____	_____

Managing and Organizing the Classroom

To what extent does your reading program exhibit each of the following?

	Sufficiently Covered	Needs Improvement
17. Variety of grouping procedures to help students learn.	_____	_____
18. Efficient class management to enhance student learning.	_____	_____

BECOMING A RESEARCHER

A researcher? We are sure your first thought is that this role is reserved exclusively for university professors, not classroom teachers. Such is not the case—a growing number of classroom teachers nationwide are conducting research to improve their teaching. Teachers active in looking at teaching and learning are able to gain new insights, bring about positive change in their classrooms, and feel more in control of their professional lives. Olson (1990) notes the following six advantages to teachers doing research:

1. Reduces the gap between research findings and classroom practice.

2. Creates a problem-solving mindset that helps teachers when they consider other classroom dilemmas.

3. Improves teachers' instructional decision-making processes.

4. Increases the professional status of teachers.

5. Helps empower teachers to influence their own profession at classroom, district, state, and national levels.

6. Offers the overriding and ultimate advantage of providing the potential for improving the educational process for children (pp. 17–18).

Effective teachers of reading base their instructional decisions not on tradition or personal opinion but on the growing knowledge base gathered through educational research. Also, effective teachers apply, monitor, and adapt any recommended research finding to their own particular classrooms and students. Since there is no one recipe for all children and classrooms, teachers must constantly observe and study the effectiveness of instructional practice. Thus, teaching is viewed not only as a way to increase student learning but also as a learning context for teachers to study teaching itself as well. Teachers of reading naturally ask questions such as, "What if?" or "Why is it that . . . ?" about different teaching methods, strategies, materials, or grouping plans. Asking questions is the basis of the research process. Teachers' educational research begins with a question or a dilemma they are experiencing in teaching reading. Through classroom observation of events during reading instruction, teachers are in a unique position to identify questions that are conducive to further study. As researchers, they attempt to shed light on an area of interest or try to understand more objectively the relationship between certain events (for example, the use of cooperative grouping and the learning of after-reading comprehension strategies).

Once researchers identify a specific question, they formulate a design for studying the question, including: (1) students to be involved (subjects); (2) treatment (that is, technique, activity, grouping plan) to be applied; (3) plan to collect information or data; (4) plan to analyze and interpret data; and (5) plan to share the results and reflect on possible changes in the classroom.

The research process is a team venture, not an individual one. Combining the talents of teachers, central-office personnel concerned with research, and university personnel makes this process both rewarding and invigorating. Individuals do not need a high degree of expertise in research and evaluation to conduct research; they need only the desire to track down answers to their questions and hunches about teaching reading.

Becoming involved in the research process is an exciting and insightful adventure.

TEACHER INDUCTION PROGRAMS

At the present time, most states and school districts have in place systematic programs to assist teachers entering the profession. The first few years of teaching have been referred to as *induction*. Learning to apply in the real world what has been learned in the university classroom is never a smooth process (Simon, 1984). There will be many ups and downs during the first year, as is the case in other professions. Closely supervised programs have been designed to address the needs of new teachers during this induction period. New teachers are given guidance in the areas of orientation to the school's routines; the curriculum; relationships with parents, colleagues, students, and administrators; time- and classroom-management; instructional strategies; and emotional support for dealing with feelings of isolation.

The key ingredient of these induction programs is an experienced, master teacher. Often referred to as mentor teachers, they work closely with new teachers as role models, providing help and encouragement. As a means to continue to learn and grow in the teaching profession, especially in the teaching of reading, teacher induction programs are excellent. Even if individuals begin teaching in a district without a planned induction program, they are encouraged to seek out an experienced mentor and design their own personalized induction program. Coupled with their own initiative in assessing and monitoring the reading program, new teachers' participation in an induction program will help them gain much knowledge, expertise, and support in becoming a successful teacher of reading.

SUMMARY

Successful teachers continually grow in their profession; they are learners, always striving to provide the very best for their students. To accomplish this goal, teachers are encouraged to (1) communicate with school and community personnel; (2) participate in professional organizations and read the professional literature; and (3) assess and monitor teaching and program effectiveness. Teachers of reading need to base their instructional decisions not on tradition or personal opinion but on the growing knowledge base gathered through educational research. Teachers must stay up-to-date and remain active in their profession. One excellent way to remain active is to become involved in the research process in their own classrooms. Most important, teachers of reading need to monitor their effectiveness and to collaborate with other professionals and parents to design meaningful learning experiences for students.

Discussion Questions and Student Projects: Growing in Your Profession

1. Invite a local representative of the International Reading Association to speak to your class. Be prepared to ask questions including the following: What are the goals of the organization on the state and local levels? Is IRA open only to reading teachers? Why should I be involved with IRA on a local level? Are local members involved in conducting classroom research?

2. Invite the administrator of a local literacy council or of RIF (Reading Is Fundamental) or another federal program to speak to your class. Ask the administrator to explain the program, the characteristics of the community and its values, and how teachers can become involved in the community.

3. While teaching a reading lesson, ask one of your peers to complete a participation guide to assess your questioning skills. Using a seating chart, your peer will place a check mark (✓) in the box of each student who answers a question. After the lesson summarize and analyze the results with your peer. Did you include all students in the lesson? Why or why not? What will you do differently in your next lesson?

4. What are the constraints to becoming involved with the community? Parents? Professional organizations? What are some strategies to deal with these constraints?

Appendices

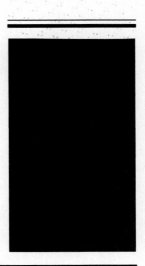

Appendix
A

Comprehension Strategies Summarized

Reciprocal Teaching

Reciprocal teaching is a teaching technique designed to improve students' comprehension abilities in reading expository text.* The technique involves teachers modeling comprehension strategies, followed by the students themselves taking over the teaching role. Four comprehension tasks are used in reciprocal teaching:

1. Developing questions.

2. Summarizing a section of text.

3. Clarifying difficult parts.

4. Predicting what the next section will discuss.

After reading a portion of a chapter, the teachers model each of the four comprehension tasks to students. When students feel comfortable with the four tasks, the students themselves become the teachers and complete the four tasks on the next section of text. The teachers assume the student role but also monitor the students' performance and provide needed feedback and encouragement.

* Source: A.S. Palinscar and A.L. Brown, "Reciprocal Teaching of Comprehension-Fostering and Comprehension-Monitoring Activities," *Cognition and Instruction* 1 (1984): 117–75.

Semantic Mapping

A semantic map is a visual technique for teaching new vocabulary or concepts by showing the relationships among words. McNeil (1984) summarizes the reasoning behind semantic mapping by stating, "The making of a semantic map is a procedure for building a bridge between the known and the new. The map provides the teacher with information on what the pupils know about a topic and gives the pupils anchor points to which the new concepts they will encounter can be attached" (p. 10). The usual procedure for constructing a map is the selection of a key word or concept from an upcoming story or chapter and brainstorming related words to form various categories. The teachers design visual displays showing the key word and its relationship to related words and categories. They can design semantic maps before reading a selection and revise the maps after reading to show new words and relationships. Discussing the maps with students has been shown to be a key ingredient to the effectiveness of semantic mapping (Stahl & Vancil, 1986). An example of a semantic map is shown on page 191.

K-W-L

The K-W-L instructional strategy developed by Ogle is designed to capitalize on students' knowledge of a topic before reading and to promote more active reading of expository text.* The letters *K, W,* and *L* stand for the three instructional steps of "assessing what I *K*now, determining what I *W*ant to know, and checking what I *L*earned from my reading." Students use a worksheet to record their own responses to the three areas as the lesson progresses. In the first step, *K,* teachers brainstorm with students what the students already know about the topic at hand. Next, the teachers help students group what they know into categories. In the second step, *W,* the teachers guide the students to generate questions the students would like answered in their reading. In the last step, *L,* students write down what they learned from their reading.

Question-Answer Relationships (QARs)

The QAR strategy focuses on helping students to identify the source of information required in answering comprehension

* Source: D.M. Ogle, "K-W-L: A Teaching Model That Develops Active Reading of Expository Text," *The Reading Teacher* 39 (1986): 564–70.

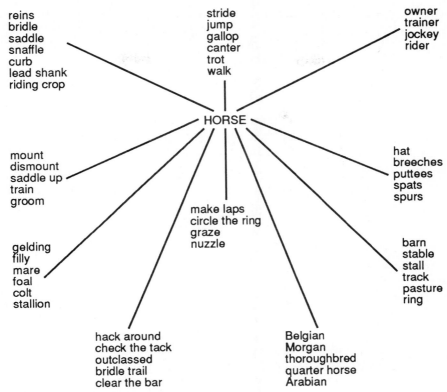

Semantic map for the word *horse.*
From D.D. Johnson and P.D. Pearson, *Teaching Reading Vocabulary,* 2nd ed. (New York: Holt, Rinehart & Winston, 1984).

questions. Sources of information can be the text itself (in the book) or the readers' background knowledge (in their heads). Using the text as the primary source of information, readers may have to identify explicitly stated information or read between the lines and integrate ideas to answer the questions. Most of the time broad questions or questions divergent in nature signal the source of information to be the readers themselves or a combination of reader background knowledge and text information. It is recommended that teachers use modeling and supervised practice to directly teach students each question-answer relationship and how to tell the difference between them. Raphael states, "QARs can be useful both as a teacher tool for conceptualizing and developing comprehension questions and as a student tool for locating information and making decisions about use of the text and background knowledge" (p. 521). In QARs, students are taught the following four relationships and mnemonics between a question, the text, and the readers' own background knowledge:

1. Right there: The answer to a question can be found right there in the text.

2. Think and search: The answer requires the student to search the text for information and to think about various pieces of information to arrive at the answer.

3. Author and you: The answer requires both information from the text and the readers' background of experiences.

4. On my own: The answer to a question is not in the text but lies within the readers.*

Expository Text Structures

Text structure is the organizational pattern in which ideas are presented to the reader. Unlike narrative text, which usually follows a simple structure, expository text can be written in several different organizational patterns.† Each type of pattern needs to be directly taught to students, and a variety of practice situations should be provided. Teaching students how to identify the various types of organizational structures while reading silently will help students better understand what they are reading. The following are six different types of expository text structure:

1. Descriptive;

2. Enumerative;

3. Sequence;

4. Cause/effect;

5. Comparison/contrast;

6. Problem/solution.

---

* Sources: T.E. Raphael, "Question-Answering Strategies for Children," *The Reading Teacher* 36 (1982): 186–91; T.E. Raphael, "Teaching Question-Answer Relationships, Revisited," *The Reading Teacher* 39 (1986): 516–22.

† Source: J.A. Piccolo, "Expository Text Structure: Teaching and Learning Strategies," *The Reading Teacher* 40 (1987): 838–47.

QUESTIONING CATEGORY	BLOOM'S CATEGORY	STUDENT ACTIVITY	TYPICAL STEM WORDS
LOWER LEVEL	Knowledge	Remembering: Facts, Terms, Definitions Concepts, Principles.	What?, List, Name, Define, Describe.
	Compre-hension	Understanding the meaning of material.	Explain, Interpret, Summarize, Give examples..., Predict, Translate.
	Application	Selecting a concept or skill and using it to solve a problem.	Compute, Solve, Apply, Modify, Construct.
HIGHER LEVEL	Analysis	Breaking material down into its parts and explaining the hierarchical relations.	How does...apply? Why does...work? How does...relate to...? What distinctions can be made about...and...?
	Synthesis	Producing something orig-inal after having broken the material down into its component parts.	How do the data support...? How would you design an experi-ment which investigates...? What predictions can you make based upon the data?
	Evaluation	Making a judgment based upon a pre-established set of criteria.	What judgments can you make about...? Compare and contrast ...criteria for...?

Constructing classroom questions. A summary of Bloom's taxonomy and breakdown be-tween lower- and higher-level questions.

From Stephanie S. Goodwin et al., *Effective Classroom Questioning* (Urbana-Champaign: University of Illinois Office of Instruction Resources/Course Development Division, 1980), p. 5.

Appendix

B

Cooperative Grouping Guidelines

Step 1: Select a lesson.
What about spelling? A page of story problems? Editing a paragraph? Comprehension questions? A science lab activity?

Step 2: Make decisions.
Select the group size. This will vary according to the resources you need in the group, the skills of the students working in groups, and the needs of the task. Experiment and find out what size works in your situation.

Assign students to groups. Heterogeneous groups have the potential for the most power. Differences among group members make the group function.

Arrange the classroom. Chairs and desks should be arranged in small clusters. Groups should be separated from each other as much as possible.

Provide the appropriate materials. Each group can have a set of materials or each group member can have different materials that relate to the task.

Step 3: Set the lesson.
State, in language your students understand:

A. a clear and specific task statement;

B. the group goal (positive interdependence);

    C. the criteria for success as a group;

    D. specific behaviors expected (for example, everyone participating, staying in group, good listening skills).

Step 4: Monitor and process.
Be sure you always monitor. If appropriate, use other observers (students, other teachers) as well. Be sure to clarify:

    A. the way observers will know that a group member is evidencing an expected behavior;

    B. who will observe and the observation form that will be used;

    C. the way data will be fed back to students.

Step 5: Intervene to solve problems and teach skills.
There will be problems. Stop the students and teach them the skills you see them needing. Turn problems back to the group to solve; act as a consultant.

Step 6: Evaluate outcomes.
Each student gets the grade his or her group received. Remember that you are evaluating how well the students learned the material or accomplished the task *and* how well they helped each other. It is also a good idea to make notes about students of special interest and to suggest ways to improve the lesson next time.

Source: D.W. Johnson and R.T. Johnson, *Promoting Constructive Student-Student Relationships Through Cooperative Learning* (Minneapolis: The Cooperative Learning Center, 1980), p. 70.

Newbery
and Caldecott
Award-Winning
Books

Newbery Award Books

Year	Title	Author
1922	*The Story of Mankind*	van Loon
1923	*The Voyages of Dr. Dolittle*	Lofting
1924	*The Dark Frigate*	Hawes
1925	*Tales from Silver Lands*	Finger
1926	*Shen of the Sea*	Christmas
1927	*Smoky the Cowhorse*	James
1928	*Gay Neck*	Mujkerji
1929	*Hitty, Her First Hundred Years*	Field
1930	*The Trumpeter of Krakow*	Kelly
1931	*The Cat Who Went to Heaven*	Coatsworth
1932	*Waterless Mountain*	Armer
1933	*Young Fu of the Upper Yangtze*	Lewis
1934	*Invincible Louisa: Anniversary Edition*	Meigs
1935	*Dobry*	Shannon
1936	*Caddie Woodlawn*	Brink
1937	*Roller Skates*	Sawyer
1938	*The White Stag*	Seredy
1939	*Thimble Summer*	Enright
1940	*Daniel Boone*	Daugherty
1941	*Call It Courage*	Sperry
1942	*Matchlock Gun*	Edmonds
1943	*Adam of the Road*	Gray
1944	*Johnny Tremain*	Forbes
1945	*Rabbit Hill*	Lawson

Year	*Title*	*Author*
1946	*Strawberry Girl*	Lenski
1947	*Miss Hickory*	Bailey
1948	*The Twenty-One Balloons*	du Bois
1949	*King of the Wind*	Henry
1950	*The Door in the Wall*	de Angeli
1951	*Amos Fortune, Free Man*	Yates
1952	*Ginger Pye*	Estes
1953	*The Secret of the Andes*	Clark
1954	*And Now Miguel*	Krumgold
1955	*The Wheel on the School*	de Jong
1956	*Carry On, Mr. Bowditch*	Latham
1957	*Miracles on Maple Hill*	Sorensen
1958	*Rifles for Waitie*	Keith
1959	*Witch of Blackbird Pond*	Speare
1960	*Onion John*	Krumgold
1961	*Island of the Blue Dolphins*	O'Dell
1962	*Bronze Bow*	Speare
1963	*A Wrinkle in Time*	L'Engle
1964	*It's Like This, Cat*	Neville
1965	*Shadow of a Bull*	Wojciechowska
1966	*I, Juan de Pareja*	de Trevino
1967	*Up a Road Slowly*	Hunt
1968	*From the Mixed-up Files of Mrs. Basil E. Frankweiler*	Konigsburg
1969	*The High King*	Alexander
1970	*Sounder*	Armstrong
1971	*Summer of the Swans*	Byars
1972	*Mrs. Frisby and the Rats of NIMH*	O'Brien
1973	*Julie of the Wolves*	George
1974	*The Slave Dancer*	Fox
1975	*M. C. Higgins, The Great*	Hamilton
1976	*The Grey King*	Cooper
1977	*Roll of Thunder, Hear My Cry*	Taylor
1978	*Bridge to Terabithia*	Paterson
1979	*The Westing Game*	Raskin
1980	*A Gathering of Days: A New England Girl's Journal, 1830–1832*	Blos
1981	*Jacob Have I Loved*	Paterson
1982	*William Blake's Inn*	Willard & Provenson
1983	*Dear Mr. Henshaw*	Cleary
1984	*Dicey's Song*	Voigt

Year	Title	Author
1985	*Hero and the Crown*	McKinley
1986	*Sarah, Plain and Tall*	MacLachlan
1987	*The Whipping Boy*	Fleischman, S.
1988	*Lincoln: A Photobiography*	Freedman
1989	*Joyful Noises*	Fleischman, P.
1990	*Number the Stars*	Lowry
1991	*Maniac Magee*	Spinelli
1992	SHILOE	

Caldecott Award Books

Year	Title	Author
1938	*Animals of the Bible*	Lathrop
1939	*Mei Li*	Handforth
1940	*Abraham Lincoln*	d'Aulaire
1941	*They Were Strong and Good*	Lawson
1942	*Make Way for Ducklings*	McCloskey
1943	*Little House*	Burton
1944	*Many Moons*	Thurber & Slobodkin
1945	*Prayer for a Child*	Field & Jones
1946	*Rooster Crown*	Petersham
1947	*Little Island*	MacDonald & Weisgard
1948	*White Snow, Bright Snow*	Tresselt & Duvoisin
1949	*Big Snow*	Hader
1950	*Song of the Swallows*	Politi
1951	*The Egg Tree*	Milhous
1952	*Finders Keepers*	Nicolas
1953	*The Biggest Bear*	Ward
1954	*Madeline's Rescue*	Bemelmans
1955	*Cinderella*	Brown
1956	*Frog Went A-Courtin'*	Langstaff & Rojankovsky
1957	*A Tree Is Nice*	Udry & Simont
1958	*Time of Wonder*	McCloskey
1959	*Chanticleer and the Fox*	Cooney
1960	*Nine Days to Christmas*	Ets & Labastida
1961	*Baboushka and the Three Kings*	Robbins
1962	*Once a Mouse*	Brown
1963	*The Snowy Day*	Keats

Year	*Title*	*Author*
1964	*Where the Wild Things Are*	Sendak
1965	*May I Bring a Friend?*	de Regniers
1966	*Always Room for One More*	Leadhas & Hogrogian
1967	*Sam Bangs & Moonshine*	News
1968	*Drummer Hoff*	Emberley
1969	*Fool of the World and the Flying Ship*	Ransome
1970	*Sylvester and the Magic Pebble*	Steig
1971	*A Story, a Story*	Haley
1972	*One Fine Day*	Hogrogian
1973	*The Funny Little Woman*	Mosel
1974	*Duffy and the Devil*	Zemach
1975	*Arrow to the Sun*	McDermott
1976	*Why Mosquitoes Buzz in People's Ears*	Aardema
1977	*Ashanti to Zulu: African Traditions*	Musgrove
1978	*Noah's Ark*	Spier
1979	*The Girl Who Loved Wild Horses*	Goble
1980	*The Ox-Cart Man*	Hall & Cooney
1981	*Fables*	Lobel
1982	*Jumanji*	Van Allsburg
1983	*Shadow*	Brown
1984	*The Glorious Flight*	Provenson
1985	*Saint George and the Dragon*	Hodges & Human
1986	*Polar Express*	Van Allsburg
1987	*Hey Al*	Yorinks & Egielski
1988	*Owl Moon*	Yolen & Schoenherr
1989	*Song and Dance Man*	Ackerman & Gammell
1990	*Lon Po Po*	Young
1991	*Black and White*	Macaulay
1992	Tuesday	

Johnson's
Basic
Vocabulary
for Beginning
Reading

Johnson's First-Grade Words

a	day	I	off	table
above	days	if	old	than
across	did	I'm	one	that
after	didn't	in	open	the
again	do	into	or	then
air	don't	is	out	there
all	door	it	over	these
am	down	its		they
American		it's		think
and	end		past	this
are		just	play	those
art	feet		point	three
as	find	keep	put	time
ask	first	kind		to
at	five		really	today
	for	let	red	too
back	four	like	right	took
be		little	room	top
before	gave	look	run	two
behind	get	love		
big	girl		said	under
black	give	make	saw	up
book	go	making	school	
boy	God	man	see	very
but	going	may	seen	
	gone	me	she	want
came	good	men	short	wanted
can	got	miss	six	was
car		money	so	way
children	had	more	some	we
come	hand	most	something	well
could	hard	mother	soon	went
	has	Mr.	still	what
	have	must		when
	he	my		where
	help			which
	her	name		who
	here	never		why
	high	new		will
	him	night		with
	his	no		work
	home	not		
	house	now		year
	how			years
				yet
				you
				your

Johnson's Second-Grade Words

able	different	last	real	water
about	does	leave	road	were
almost	done	left		west
alone		light	same	while
already	each	long	say	whole
always	early		says	whose
America	enough	made	set	wife
an	even	many	should	women
another	ever	mean	show	world
any	every	might	small	would
around	eyes	morning	sometimes	
away		Mrs.	sound	
	face	much	started	
because	far	music	street	
been	feel		sure	
believe	found	need		
best	from	next	take	
better	front	nothing	tell	
between	full	number	their	
board			them	
both	great	of	thing	
bought	group	office	things	
by		on	thought	
	hands	only	through	
called	having	other	together	
change	head	our	told	
church	heard	outside	town	
city		own	turn	
close	idea			
company		part	until	
cut	knew	party	us	
	know	people	use	
		place	used	
		plan		
		present		

Source: D.D. Johnson and P.D. Pearson, *Teaching Reading Vocabulary,* 2nd ed.
(New York: Holt, Rinehart and Winston, 1984).

Appendix
E

Phonic Generalizations

MAJOR LETTER-SOUND CORRESPONDENCES

For each pattern sample, words are used to illustrate the letter-sound relationships that need to be learned. Occasionally a rule is given.

Consonants

b—book	l—lemon	r—roll	x—xylophone
d—dance	m—money	s—sit *or* was	exam
f—funny	n—new	t—top *or* nation	tax
h—heart	p—party	v—violin	y—yes
j—job	qu—queen	w—water	z—zebra
k—king			

Other Consonants

c—cent	c—cat
city	cot
cycle	cup

Rule: *C* sounds like *s* before *e, i,* and *y* and sounds like *k* elsewhere.

g—gem	g—game
agile	gone
gym	guild

Rule: *G* sounds like *j* before *e, i,* and *y* and sounds like *g* elsewhere.

Double Consonants

digraphs	sh—shoe	th—thin	ch—chew
	ph—photo	this	choir
	ng—song	wh—while	chef

doubles	bb—rabble	nn—funny
	dd—ladder	pp—happen
	ff—jiffy	rr—narrow
	ll—belly	vv—savvy
	mm—dimmer	zz—dizzy
	cc—buccaneer	gg—egg
	accept	suggest

Rule: Except for *cc* and *gg*, two identical consonants have one sound.

blends	bl—black	br—brown	sc—scat
	cl—clue	cr—cry	scr—screen
	fl—flap	dr—draw	sm—small
	gl—glass	fr—friend	sn—snow
	pl—play	gr—ground	sp—spot
	sl—slow	pr—proud	squ—squeak
		tr—trap	st—stump
			sw—swing

silent letters	kn—knee	wr—wrong
	mb—comb	ten—fasten

Vowels

i—if	a—act	o—hot
mild	about	of
bird	ape	note
	want	off
	call	for
	star	
u—much	e—bed	
cute	jacket	
tube	blaze	
bull	often	
fur	she	
	her	

Rules: 1. A vowel between two consonants is usually "short": *pin, cap, hot, bug, bed.*
2. A vowel before two or more consonants is usually "short": *wish, graph, much, blotter, lettuce, happen, itch, hospital, cinder, bumper.*
3. A vowel followed by a consonant plus *e* is usually "long": *pine, date dope, cute, mete.*
4. The letter *y* sometimes is a vowel, and it has two sounds: *my, baby.*

Double Vowels

io—nation	ou—ounce	au—because
lion	though	laugh
ea—teach	soup	oo—moon
bread	would	book
great		
ai—pain	ee—see	ow—own
said	been	cow
ay—play		oi—coin

Source: R.J. Smith and D.D. Johnson, *Teaching Children to Read*, 2nd ed. (Boston: Addison-Wesley, 1980).

Explicit or Direct Instruction Guidelines

1. Daily Review and Checking Homework
   Checking homework (routine for students to check each other's papers)
   Reteaching when necessary
   Reviewing relevant past learning (may include questioning)
   Review prerequisite skills (if applicable)

2. Presentation
   Provide short statement of objectives
   Provide overview and structuring
   Proceed in small steps but at a rapid pace
   Intersperse questions within the demonstration to check for under-
   standing
   Highlight main points
   Provide sufficient illustrations and concrete examples
   Provide demonstrations and models
   When necessary, give detailed and redundant instructions and examples

3. Guided Practice
   Initial student practice takes place with teacher guidance
   High frequency of questions and overt student practice (from teacher
   and/or materials)
   Questions are directly relevant to the new content or skill
   Teacher checks for understanding (CFU) by evaluating student
   responses
   During CFU teacher gives additional explanation, processes feedback,
   or repeats explanation—where necessary
   All students have a chance to respond and receive feedback; teacher
   insures that all students participate

Prompts are provided during guided practice (where appropriate)

Initial student practice is sufficient so that students can work independently

Guided practice continues until students are firm

Guided practice is continued (usually) until a success rate of 80% is achieved

4. Correctives and Feedback

Quick, firm, and correct responses can be followed by another question or short acknowledgement of correctness (i.e., "That's right")

Hesitant correct answers might be followed by process feedback (i.e., "Yes, Linda, that's right because . . .")

Student errors indicate a need for more practice

Monitor students for systematic errors

Try to obtain a substantive response to each question

Corrections can include sustaining feedback (i.e., simplifying the question, giving clues), explaining, reviewing steps, giving process feedback, or reteaching the last steps

Try to elicit an improved response when the first one is incorrect

Guided practice and corrections continue until the teacher feels that the group can meet the objectives of the lesson

Praise should be used in moderation, and specific praise is more effective than general praise

5. Independent Practice (Seatwork)

Sufficient practice

Practice is directly relevant to skills/content taught

Practice to overlearning

Practice until responses are firm, quick, and automatic

Ninety-five percent correct rate during independent practice

Students alerted that seatwork will be checked

Students held accountable for seatwork

Actively supervise students, when possible

6. Weekly and Monthly Reviews

Systematic review of previously learned material

Include review in homework

Frequent tests

Reteaching of material missed in tests

Note: With older, more mature learners, or learners with more knowledge of the subject, the following adjustments can be made: (1) the size of the step in presentation can be larger (more material is presented at one time), (2) there is less time spent on teacher-guided practice and (3) the amount of overt practice can be decreased, replacing it with covert rehearsal, restating and reviewing.

Source: B. Rosenshine and R. Stevens, **"Teaching Functions"** in *Handbook of Research on Teaching,* M.C. Wittrock, ed. (New York: Macmillan, 1986), pp. 377–91. Copyright 1986 by the American Educational Research Association. Reprinted by permission.

Appendix

G

Features of Black English

Category*	Feature	Explanation	Written sE	Example(s) Spoken bE
Phonological	1. Final consonant cluster simplification	Words ending in a consonant cluster have the final letter of the cluster absent.	desk	"des"
	2. th sounds	(a) Initial voiced th pronounced as /d/.	that	"dat"
		(b) Medial and final voiceless th pronounced as /f/.	bathroom	"bafroom"
		(c) Medial and final voiced th pronounced as /v/.	mother	"muhver"
		(d) Final th in with pronounced /d/ or /t/.	with	"wid" "wit"
	3. Final consonant devoicing or absence.	(a) Voiced stops /b/, /d/, /g/ are pronounced like corresponding voiceless stops /p/, /t/, /k/, respectively.	fed pig	"fet" "pick"
		(b) Loss of final consonant sounds.	mad	"ma"
	4. Absence of medial consonants.	Medial consonants can be absent.	little help worry throw	"lil" "hep" "wo'y" "thow"
	5. Effect of nasal consonant.	(a) The /g/ in ing is absent. (b) Use of nasalized vowel instead of the nasal consonants.	running balloon	"runnin" "balloo" "balloom"
			rum	"ru" "run"
		(c) Short vowels "i" and "e" do not contrast.	pin and pen	"pin"
	6. str- cluster	str- clusters are pronounced /skr/.	street	"skreet"
	7. Long i	Long i is pronounced like the a in father ("ah").	time	"tahm"

Category*	Feature	Explanation	Example(s) Written sE	Spoken bE
	8. Article *an*	The article *a* is used whether the following word begins with a vowel or a consonant.	*an* *umbrella*	"a umbrella"
	9. Verb forms with *to*	When following a verb, *to* is pronounced "ta" or "a."	*have to* *went to* *going to*	"hafta" "went a" "gonna"
	10. Stress patterns	(a) Stress is placed on first syllable on some words which have second syllable stress in sE.	*umbrella*	"um-brella"
		(b) First syllable can be absent when it is unstressed.	*about*	"bout"
	11. Final *t* followed by *'s*.	When final *t* is followed by the *'s* of a contraction the *t* is not pronounced.	*it's* *what's*	"is" "whas"
	12. *ask*	In the word *ask*, the final consonant cluster is reversed.	*ask*	"aks"
	13. Consonant *v*.	The consonant *v* is pronounced with a voiced bilabial fricative which is unknown in sE. It sounds somewhat like /b/ or /w/.	*over*	"ober" "ower"
	14. *don't*	This word can lose its initial sound (as well as its final sound, see Feature 1).	*don't*	"on"
Morphological	15. Loss of *-ed* suffix	The past tense marker *-ed* is absent.	*missed*	"miss"
	16. The present tense suffix	The present tense marker *-s* used for the third person singular is absent.	*He wants*	"He want"
	17. Plurals	The plural marker *-s* is absent.	*toys*	"toy"

Syntactical

18. Possessives	The possessive marker 's is absent.	*boy's*	"boy"
19. Irregular Past Tense	Irregular past tense forms are replaced by present tense forms.	*said*	"say"
20. The past participle	With irregular verbs, the past tense and the past participle may interchange.	*He has come.* *He has taken it.*	"He has came." "He taken it."
21. The verb *to be*	(a) The verb forms *is* and *was* are used for all persons and numbers.	*They're running.*	"They's runnin'."
	(b) The verb forms of *to be* are often missing.	*She is tired.* *They are busy.*	"She tired." "They busy."
22. Invariant *be*	*Be* is used as a main verb, regardless of person and number.	*Sometimes he is busy.*	"Sometime he be busy."
23. Auxiliary deletions	Auxiliary verb forms are absent.	*He is going to school.* *She'll have to go home.*	"He goin' a school." "She have to go home."
24. Negation	More than one negative marker is used.	*He doesn't know anything.*	"He 'on' know nothin'."
25. Relative clauses	(a) In relative clauses, relative pronouns are absent.	*That's the dog that bit me.*	"Tha's the dog bit me."
	(b) In relative clauses, *what* replaces relative pronoun.	*That's the dog that bit me.*	"Tha's the dog wha' bit me."

Category*	Feature	Explanation	Example(s) Written sE	Example(s) Spoken bE
	26. Question inversion	(a) Indirect questions follow direct question rules.	*His mother asked why he was late.*	"His mother aks why was he late?"
		(b) Direct questions follow indirect question rules.	*Why did he take it?*	"Why he did take it?"
	27. *There* constructions	Existential or expletive *there* is replaced by *it*.	*There was a convertible outside.*	"It was a convertible outside."
	28. Pronominal apposition	A noun and its pronoun are the subject of a sentence.	*His mother threw out the balloon.*	"His mother, she th'ew out the balloon."
	29. Use of *at* after *where*	Questions that begin with *where* end with *at*.	*Where is she?*	"Where she at?"
	30. Undifferentiated pronouns	Standard English nominative forms of personal pronouns are used to show possession.	*That's his book.*	"Tha's he book."
	31. Reflexives	Pronouns formed with the possessive form of the personal pronoun plus *self*.	*himself*	"hisself"
	32. Demonstratives	The use of *them* when standard English requires *those*.	*I want some of those candies.*	"I want some a them candies."

* Semantic features, because of frequent changes, are omitted from list.

Source: Bonnie Lass, "The Relationship Between the Oral Language of Black English Speakers and Their Reading Achievements." Doctoral dissertation, University of Illinois, 1976 (unpublished).

Appendix

H

Some Spanish Language Features That May Cause Problems in Reading English

Category	Feature	Explanation	Examples	
			Written English	Spoken English
Phonological	/i/ = /ē/	Short i is pronounced as long e.	sin ship	"seen" "sheep"
	/ē/ = /i/ /ā/ = /e/	Long e is pronounced as short i. Long a is pronounced as short e.	sleep late sale	"slip" "let" "sell"
	/v/ = /b/	/v/ and /b/ are represented by only one sound in Spanish, which is close to the sound /b/.	very vote valentine	"bury" "boat" "ballentine"
	/ch/ = /sh/	The Spanish pronunciation of /ch/ sounds like /sh/ to English speakers.	chip much teacher	"ship" "mush" "tee-shir(t)"
	/th/	Initial voiced /th/ is pronounced as /d/ and final unvoiced /th/ is pronounced /s/.	this with	"dis" "wis"
	/j/ = /y/ or /ch/	J is pronounced as /y/ or /ch/, while initial /y/ is pronounced in an approximation of /j/.	job just	"yob" or "chob" "yust" or "chust"
	/y/ = /j/		yo-yo yes	"jo-jo" "jes"
	Absence of final consonants	Because /p/, /t/, /k/ and /f/ do not appear in the final position in Spanish words, these sounds are often omitted from English ones. This is particularly true with multisyllabic words or words in phrases.	hate economic student get off climb up	"hay" "economy" "studen" "get o'" "climb u'"
	Final consonant cluster simplification	Spanish has no final consonant clusters so there is pronunciation difficulty with words ending in clusters.	cats hopped moved	"cat" or "cass" "hop" "move" or "mood"

Morphological	Initial s blends	Spanish has no initial consonant cluster beginning with /s/. There is a tendency for Spanish speakers to make a syllable out of an /s/ blend by adding /e/ to its beginning.	*sleep* *smile* *skin*	"esleep" "esmile" "eskin"
	Superlatives	In English we inflect comparative adjectives (large, larger, largest). In Spanish, other comparative adjectives and articles are added to the first (grande, más grande, el más grande).	*larger* *largest*	"more large" or "more larger", "the more large"
	Possessive	There is no possessive case form in Spanish; "John's hat" is "El sombrero de Juan." This sometimes causes comprehension problems.	*John's hat* *the mother's cat*	"The hat of John" or "John hat", "the mother cat"
	Stress	Rules are different in Spanish—second or third syllables, or marked vowels (está) are usually stressed while in English, the first syllable of a root is emphasized.	*comment* *pilot* *language*	"commént" "pilót" "langúage"
Syntactic	Future tense	In Spanish, the most common future tense employs an inflected verb. In English, the modal "will" is the most common future marker. Consequently, "will" is frequently omitted and unless there is a specific referent in the sentence (e.g., "tomorrow"), comprehension problems can result.	*She will laugh*	"She laugh"
	Conditional tense	Conditional verbs are present in Spanish but uncommon in oral language of school-aged children. Conditional markers are often omitted in verb phrases, sometimes causing difficulty with the understanding of cause-and-effect relationships.	*She would speak* *She may speak*	"She speak"

Category	Feature	Explanation	Examples	
			Written English	Spoken English
Syntactic	Prepositions	Spanish speakers sometimes translate prepositions into English literally when the correct preposition is idiomatic. The examples to the right are the idiomatic and literal translations of the sentence "Yo sueño con ser rico."	*I dream about being rich.*	"I dream with being rich."
	Possessive adjective	Spanish direct and indirect object pronouns come before the verb. The result for the Spanish speaker reading English may be disordered.	*He showed it to me.*	"He showed me it." "He show it me." "To me he show it."
	Negation	The Spanish word "su" means "his," "her," and "your" (formal case), so there may be some confusion among these words. Moreover, there is occasionally confusion between these adjectives and subject pronouns.	*Mary showed her mother the flower.*	"Mary showed his (or she) mother the flower."
		In Spanish a double negative is usual ("*No tengo nada*" = "He has nothing"). When reading English, where only one negative marker is used, comprehension may be affected. After reading *He has nothing* and asked "Does he have anything?", the Spanish-speaking child may reply, "Yes," because the negative was not emphatic enough.	*He has nothing.*	"He no has nothing."

Adapted from: B. Lass and B. Davis, *The Remedial Reading Handbook.* Needham, Mass.: Allyn & Bacon (1985).

Appendix

I

Teacher Practices That May Threaten Students Experiencing Difficulty in Reading

- Requiring students to read aloud in front of other children. During oral reading, teachers frequently interrupt students to correct their pronunciation, tempo, rate, and lack of appropriate inflection of expression.

- Requiring students to stand up before the class and act out parts of stories or plays that require reading difficult lines or passages in front of their peers.

- Requiring students to read from books or materials that are either too long or too hard for them and then having them reread when this serves no constructive purpose.

- Requiring students to read aloud from material that is obviously more appropriate for younger children.

- Requiring students to stop reading because they have made too many errors or appear lost or confused. At this point teachers often ask some other students to "help" the youngsters locate certain pieces of information, find the right place in the book or material, pronounce certain words, answer questions, or make more accurate interpretations.

- Requiring students to read and then, in a misguided attempt at humor, mimicking or commenting upon the quality of their reading or behavior.

- Requiring students to do the same kind of reading day after day from basal readers and to complete innumerable workbook activities in order to overcome skills deficits.

The activities frequently bore students, and boredom or lack of purpose is stressful and frustrating. The attempt to strengthen weaknesses by focusing solely on them does nothing to alter students' perceptions of themselves as poor readers. In fact, quite the opposite may be true. By constantly having to face or confront these weaknesses, students' perceived incompetencies actually may be confirmed.

- Requiring students to read material that parallels specific traumatic conditions in their lives. Bibliotherapy is appropriate in some circumstances but should be used with sensitivity so that it does not contribute to students' anxiety or feelings of inadequacy.

Source: L.M. Gentile and M.M. McMillan. *Stress and Reading Difficulties: Research, Assessment, and Intervention* (Newark: Del: International Reading Association, 1987), p. 4.

Appendix

J

Lesson Plan Forms

Lesson Focus:

Instructional Objective:

Readiness:

Step-By-Step Explanation:

Guided Practice:

Independent Practice:

Extension Activity:

Lesson Focus:

    Instructional Objective:

    Readiness:

    Step-By-Step Explanation:

    Guided Practice:

    Independent Practice:

    Extension Activity:

Lesson Focus:

Instructional Objective:

Readiness:

Step-By-Step Explanation:

Guided Practice:

Independent Practice:

Extension Activity:

Lesson Focus:

    Instructional Objective:

    Readiness:

    Step-By-Step Explanation:

    Guided Practice:

    Independent Practice:

    Extension Activity:

Lesson Focus:

Instructional Objective:

Readiness:

Step-By-Step Explanation:

Guided Practice:

Independent Practice:

Extension Activity:

Lesson Focus:

    Instructional Objective:

    Readiness:

    Step-By-Step Explanation:

    Guided Practice:

    Independent Practice:

    Extension Activity:

Lesson Focus:

Instructional Objective:

Readiness:

Step-By-Step Explanation:

Guided Practice:

Independent Practice:

Extension Activity:

Bibliography

Adams, Marilyn Jager. (1990a). *Beginning to Read: Thinking and Learning About Print.* Cambridge, MA: MIT Press.

———. (1990b). *Beginning to Read: Thinking and Learning About Print.* Summary prepared by Stahl, S.A., J. Osborn, and F. Lehr, University of Illinois at Urbana-Champaign: Center for the Study of Reading and The Reading Research and Education Center.

Anderson, L.M., C.M. Evertson, and J.E. Brophy. (1979). "An Experimental Study of Effective Teaching in First-Grade Reading Groups." *The Elementary School Journal* 79: 193–223.

Anderson, R.C., E.H. Hiebert, J.A. Scott, and I. Wilkinson, eds. (1985). *Becoming a Nation of Readers: The Report of the Commission on Reading.* Contract No. 400-83-0057. Washington, D.C.: National Institute of Education.

Balajthy, E. (1986). *Microcomputers in Reading and Language Arts.* Englewood Cliffs, NJ: Prentice-Hall.

Becher, R.M. (1985). "Parent Involvement and Reading Achievement: A Review of Research and Implications for Practice." *Childhood Education* 62: 44–49.

Berliner, D.C. (1981). "Academic Learning Time and Reading Achievement." In J.T. Guthrie, ed., *Comprehension and Teaching: Research Reviews,* 203–26. Newark, DE: International Reading Association.

Blanton, William E., Karen D. Wood, and Gary B. Moorman. (1990). "The Role of Purpose in Reading Instruction." *The Reading Teacher* 43(7): 486–93.

California State Department of Education. (1988a). *Annotated Recommended Readings in Literature: Kindergarten through Grade Eight.* Sacramento, CA.

———. (1988b). *Handbook for Planning an Effective Literature Program*. Sacramento, CA.

Corrigan, D. (1982). "Curriculum Issues in the Preparation of Teachers." Address delivered at the World Assembly of the International Council on Education for Teaching, Rome, Italy.

Fisher, C.W., R.S. Marliave, and N.N. Filby. (1979). "Improving Teaching by Increasing 'Academic Learning Time.'" *Educational Leadership* 37: 53–54.

Gambrell, L.B. (1980). "Think-Time: Implications for Reading Instruction." *The Reading Teacher* 34(2): 143–46.

Gates, A.I. (1937). "The Necessary Age for Beginning Reading." *The Elementary School Journal* 37: 497–508.

Gentile, L.M., and M.M. McMillan. (1984). "Stress as a Factor in Reading Difficulties: From Research to Practice." Paper presented at the American Reading Forum National Conference, Orlando, FL.

———. (1987). *Stress and Reading Difficulties: Research, Assessment, and Intervention*. Newark, DE: International Reading Association.

———. (1989). "Literacy Through Literature: Motivating 'At Risk' Students to Read and Write." Paper presented at the College Reading Association Annual Conference, Philadelphia, PA.

Good, T., and J. Brophy (1987). *Looking in Classrooms*. 4th ed. New York: Harper & Row.

Guthrie, J.T. (1977). "Research Views: Recreating Successful Reading Programs." *The Reading Teacher* 30(8): 952–55.

Harris, T.L., and R.E. Hodges, eds. (1981). *A Dictionary of Reading and Related Terms*. Newark, DE: International Reading Association.

Heilman, A.W., T.R. Blair, and W.H. Rupley. (1990). *Principles and Practices of Teaching Reading*, 7th ed. Columbus, OH: Merrill Publishing Company.

Hofmeister, A. (1984). *Microcomputer Applications in the Classroom*. New York: Holt, Rinehart and Winston.

Huck, C.S., S. Helper, and J. Hickman. (1979). *Children's Literature in the Elementary School*. 4th ed. New York: Holt, Rinehart and Winston.

Hunt, L.C. (1970). "The Effect of Self-Selection, Interest and Motivation upon Independent, Instructional, and Frustration Levels." *The Reading Teacher* 24(2): 146–51.

Johnson, D., and R. Johnson. (1974). "Instructional Goal Structure: Cooperative, Competitive, or Individualistic." *Review of Educational Research* 44: 213–40.

Johnson, D.D., and P.D. Pearson. (1984). *Teaching Reading Vocabulary*. 2nd ed. New York: Holt, Rinehart and Winston.

Maring, G.H., and J. Magelky (1990). "Effective Communication: Key to Parent/Community Involvement." *The Reading Teacher* 43: 606–07.

Mavrogene, N.A. (1990). "Helping Parents Help Their Children Become Literate." *Young Children* 45: 4–9.

McNeil, J.D. (1987). *Reading Comprehension: New Directions for Classroom Practice.* 2nd ed. Glenview, IL: Scott, Foresman and Company.

Nagy, W., and P. Herman. (1987). "Breadth and Depth of Vocabulary Knowledge: Implications for Acquisition and Instruction." In M. McKeown and M. Curtis, eds., *The Nature of Vocabulary Acquisition.* Hillsdale, NJ: Erlbaum.

Norton, D.E. (1991). *Through the Eyes of the Child: An Introduction to Children's Literature.* 3rd ed. Columbus, OH: Merrill Publishing Company.

Olson, M.W. (1990). "The Teacher as Researcher: A Historical Perspective." In M.W. Olson, ed., *Opening the Door to Classroom Research.* Newark, DE: International Reading Association.

Palinscar, A.S., and A.L. Brown. (1986). "Interactive Teaching to Promote Independent Learning from Text." *The Reading Teacher* 39(8): 771–77.

Raphael, T.E. (1984). "Teaching Learners About Sources of Information for Answering Comprehension Questions." *Journal of Reading* 27(4): 303–11.

Rasinski, T., and A.D. Fredericks. (1989). "Can Parents Make a Difference?" *The Reading Teacher* 43: 84–85.

_____. (1990). "Working with Parents: The Best Reading Advice for Parents." *The Reading Teacher* 43: 344–45.

Raths, L.E., S. Wassermann, A. Jonas, and A.M. Rothstein. (1986). *Teaching for Thinking: Theory, Strategies, and Activities for the Classroom.* New York: Teachers College Press, Columbia University.

Rich, D. (1988). "Bridging the Parent Gap in Education Reform." *Educational Horizons* 66: 90–92.

Rosenshine, B.V. (1979). "Content, Time, and Direct Instruction." In P. Peterson and H. Walbers, eds., *Research on Teaching Concepts, Findings, and Implications,* 28–56. Berkeley, CA: McCutchan Publishing Corp.

Rumelhart, D. (1976). *Toward an Interactive Model of Reading.* Technical Report No. 56. San Diego: Center for Human Information Processing, University of California.

Schmidtmann, N.K. (1989). "The Media Specialist and the Future of Literate America: The Task Ahead." *Catholic Library World* 60: 206–11.

Simon, V. (1984). "Perceived Problems of Beginning Teachers." *Review of Educational Research* 54: 143–78.

Spiegel, D.L. (1981). *Reading for Pleasure: Guidelines.* Reading Aids Series. Newark, DE: ERIC Clearinghouse on Reading and Communication Skills and International Reading Association.

Stauffer, R.G. (1975). *Directing the Reading-Thinking Process.* New York: Harper & Row.

Strickland, D.S., J.T. Feeley, and S.B. Wepner. (1987). *Using Computers in the Teaching of Reading.* New York: Teachers College Press.

Trelease, J. (1989). *The New Read-Aloud Handbook.* New York: Penguin.

Turner, S. (1989). "Bad Books for Children—What Are They?" *Emergency Librarian* 16: 15–18.

Vukelich, C. (1984). "Parents' Role in the Reading Process: A Review of Practical Suggestions and Ways to Communicate with Parents." *The Reading Teacher* 37: 472–77.

Wahl, A. (1988). "Ready . . . Set . . . Role: Parents' Role in Early Reading." *The Reading Teacher* 42: 228, 231.

Wittrock, M.C. (1987). "Process-Oriented Measures of Comprehension." *The Reading Teacher* 40(8): 734–37.

Index

Page numbers in italics refer to figures or tables.

Permissions

Model lesson plan for the basal story "Daisy's Surprise," by Dolly Celubash (pp. 89–106), adapted from *HBJ Reading Program–Sand Castles,* Teacher's Edition, Level 5, Laureate Ed., by B. Cullinan et al., copyright © 1989 by Harcourt Brace Jovanovich, Inc. Reprinted by permission of the publisher.

Appendix B, "Cooperative Grouping Guidelines" (pp. 194–195), reprinted by permission of the authors. In *Circles of Learning,* by David W. Johnson, Roger Johnson, and E. Holubec, published by Interaction Book Company, Edina, Minn. (1990).

Appendix D, "Johnson's Basic Vocabulary for Beginning Reading" (pp. 200–202), from *Teaching Reading Vocabulary,* 2nd ed., by Dale Johnson, copyright © 1984 by Holt, Rinehart and Winston, Inc. Reprinted by permission of the publisher.

Appendix E, "Phonic Generalizations" (pp. 203–205), from R.J. Smith and D.D. Johnson, *Teaching Children to Read,* 2nd edition, published by, and reprinted with kind permission of, Addison-Wesley Publishing Company, Menlo Park, Calif. (1980).

Appendix F, "Explicit or Direct Instruction Guidelines" (pp. 206–207), from "Teaching Functions" by B. Rosenshine and R. Stevens. Reprinted with permission of Macmillan Publishing Company from *Handbook of Research on Teaching,* 3rd ed., Merlin C. Wittrock, ed. Copyright © 1986 by the American Education Research Association (pp. 371–391).

About the Authors

TIMOTHY R. BLAIR is Assistant Dean of the College of Education at the University of Central Florida, located in Orlando. Previously Professor of Reading Education at Texas A&M University, Dr. Blair is a former elementary classroom teacher, and has taught reading at the elementary, middle, and high-school levels. He is the author of a text on teacher effectiveness, co-author of three college textbooks on the teaching of reading and related topics, and has written numerous articles for professional journals. He received his B.S. (in Elementary Education) and M.S. (in Reading) from Central Connecticut State University; his Ph.D. (in Early Childhood and Elementary Education, with a major in Reading) was awarded by the University of Illinois. He has been a keynote speaker at numerous national and state conferences.

EDWARD C. TURNER is Associate Professor of Reading in the Department of Instruction and Curriculum at the University of Florida, located in Gainesville. He has taught elementary-level students and has been a remedial reading teacher, and for four years directed the Teacher Corps Project at the University of Florida, training teachers to work in multicultural schools. Dr. Turner is much in demand as a director of in-service workshops. He also speaks frequently to parent groups and at national and state conferences. He has been honored repeatedly for his work as both a teacher and advisor. Dr. Turner received his B.S. (in Elementary Education) and M.S. (in Administration and Supervision) from the State University College at Buffalo, New York, while his Ph.D. (in Reading) was awarded by Michigan State University.

BARBARA A. SCHAUDT is Associate Professor of Reading, and Coordinator of Multiple Subjects Field Experiences, in the School of Education at California State University, Bakersfield. Her teaching experience includes work with adult literacy, the elementary and high-school Title I levels, and activity as a clinical reading specialist. She has presented papers at major conferences including those of the International Reading Association and the California Reading Association, and has written articles for professional journals such as *The Reading Teacher*. Dr. Schaudt earned her B.S. (in Child Development and Teaching) at Michigan State University, her M.A. (in Reading/Language Arts) at Oakland University, and her Ph.D. (in Curriculum and Instruction, with an emphasis in Reading) at Texas A&M University.